SEVEN LESSONS IN CONSCIOUS LIVING

SEVEN LESSONS IN CONSCIOUS LIVING

A Progressive Program
of Higher Learning and
Spiritual Practice in the
Kriya Yoga Tradition

ROY EUGENE DAVIS
A direct disciple of
Paramahansa Yogananda

CSA PRESS / Center For Spiritual Awareness

ISBN 0-87707-280-9

CSA Press, P.O. Box 7, Lakemont, Georgia 30552-0001
Telephone (706) 782-4723   Fax (706) 782-4560
E-mail csainc@csa-davis.org   Website www.csa-davis.org

CSA Press is the publishing department of Center for Spiritual Awareness.

Roy Eugene Davis, the founder-director of Center for Spiritual Awareness, was ordained by Paramahansa Yogananda (Los Angeles, California, 1951).

The international headquarters of Center for Spiritual Awareness is located in the low mountain region of northeast Georgia, 90 miles from Atlanta.

INTRODUCTION

A Cordial Invitation to Spiritual Fulfillment

Opinions about the meaning of life and the purposes for our being in this world are of little value. If our thoughts and actions do not enhance our lives, the lives of others, and the environment, our relatively brief sojourn in this mundane realm of temporary relationships and transitory events is wasted.

The information provided in the following pages is reliable and can be verified by practical application. Results will always be in accord with your personal vision of possibilities and attentive participation with the universal, impartial laws of cause and effect which will support your right endeavors.

If you sincerely aspire to live effectively and experience rapid, authentic spiritual growth, the philosophical principles, lifestyle guidelines, and meditation practices described in these lessons will be extremely helpful to you.

I pray that your learning and progress will be rapid and enjoyable.

ROY EUGENE DAVIS

January 2000
Lakemont, Georgia (U.S.A.)

Read a little. Meditate more. Think of God all the time.
– words of Paramahansa Yogananda to the author

How to Study and Practice for Favorable Results

- Read the table of contents on the facing page.
- Look through the following pages to familiarize yourself with the material.
- After reading lesson one, immediately apply the recommended guidelines and practices.
- Read lessons two through seven.
- When you discover a word or concept that is not defined or explained in the text, refer to the glossary. If several words or philosophical concepts in the text are new to you, it may be helpful to read the glossary before reading the lessons.
- After reading the entire text, including the glossary, devote one month to each lesson. Apply the recommended guidelines and practice the meditation techniques described in that lesson.
- This is a self-learning program. It is not necessary to discuss the material, your ideas, or your personal practices with others.

Note: If friends meet to study these lessons and meditate together, discussion for the purpose of clarifying what has been read may be of value. One or two members of the group should be appointed as coordinators to keep discussions focused on the lesson theme. Request group guideline information from the Center for Spiritual Awareness office.

CONTENTS

THE WISDOM OF PARAMAHANSA YOGANANDA

Life has to be lived; why not live it the highest way? You could look at a beautiful work of art or an ideal situation and find some fault with it. But why do that? Look for the good in all that you behold.

If you want God's guidance in your life, don't waste time in idle talk with others. Silence is the altar of Spirit.

To define yourself in terms of human limitations is to desecrate the image of God which you are.

That person is wisest who aspires to know God. That person is most successful who realizes God.

Pray like this: "Infinite God. I will reason, will, and act. Please guide my reason, will, and actions so that I may do what you would have me do."

I never allow the word "impossible" to take root in my mind; nor should you.

Let your devotion to God be like a wood fire that burns steadily for a long time; not like a straw fire that produces a bright flame then quickly goes out.

Prosperity does not mean to always have what you want. You are truly prosperous when you always have what you need.

Thinking that you are not free keeps you from being free. Cease thinking like that and you will be free.

Demonstrate compassion. While you are learning to swim in the sea of life, you can help others learn to swim.

Discard the false belief that there is a separation between spiritual and material life. Perform duties skillfully. All constructive work is purifying if done with the right motive. If you sometimes fail to accomplish your purposes, don't be discouraged; that is the best time to sow the seeds of success. In everything you do, express your limitless soul qualities.

Don't go only halfway on the spiritual path; three quarters of the way; or almost to the end and then quit. Be firmly resolved to go all the way [to be Self- and God-realized].

Every day, meditate more deeply than you did the day before.

When you know [have realized] God, life is enjoyable.

LESSON ONE

PHILOSOPHY

THE KRIYA YOGA TRADITION

Austerity, study of sacred texts and application of what is learned, and surrender to God is kriya yoga.

Kriya yoga is practiced to resist, weaken, and remove all physical and mental obstacles to God-realization.

– Patanjali's yoga-sutras 2:1,2

In this spiritual enlightenment tradition, *austerity* (insightful self-analysis and disciplined thinking, feeling, and behavior) is emphasized to facilitate psychological transformation. *Study* (insightful examination) of the real nature of the soul, consciousness and its processes, and the reality of God enables one to acquire accurate knowledge and to apprehend the truth; what is real, in contrast to what was formerly presumed as real. *Surrender to God* is the letting go of the illusional sense of selfhood in favor of directly realizing (apprehending and experiencing) one's essence of being, which is pure consciousness.

Kriya (Sanskrit verb-root *kri*, to do) means "action." For the practitioner of yoga, *kriyas* are productive actions implemented to accomplish chosen purposes, and the transformative, regenerative actions which spontaneously occur in the body and mind when obvious spiritual awakening has occurred. The word *yoga* (verb-root *yug*, to join or unite) is commonly used to refer to procedures which harmonize the interactions of body, mind and soul. In the *yoga-sutras* written by Patanjali approximately two thousand years ago, the meaning is twofold: procedures to be learned and practiced; clarified states of awareness which may be experienced by attentive, knowledgeable practice.

Teachers of this kriya yoga path proclaim that it is possible, by wholesome living, the systematic development of intellectual and intuitive powers, proficient meditation practice, and the redemptive actions of grace, to experience rapid spiritual growth that culminates in illumination of consciousness in a few years. For truth seekers who once believed that many decades, perhaps incarnations, of arduous endeavor was to be their fate, being informed of the possibility that Self- and God-knowledge can be quickly realized should inspire and motivate them to be more focused, decisive, and purposeful.

Along with lifestyle regimens and spiritual practices commonly emphasized by most authentic enlightenment traditions, kriya yoga practitioners are taught several unique meditation techniques. These, when correctly practiced, elicit deep physical relaxation, calm the mind, enliven the nervous system, refine the body, and enable the skillful meditator to more easily experience superconscious (transcendent) states of awareness.

THE TEACHERS OF THIS KRIYA YOGA TRADITION

Because *kriyas* are "actions" anyone who teaches a system of yoga practice can refer to it as kriya yoga. In the tradition which I represent, instruction is always transmitted through a lineage of gurus, each of whom was taught, and empowered to teach, by a predecessor. In this way, through the centuries, the teachings have remained pure (undiluted) and the spiritual vitality imparted with them is potent. In this kriya yoga tradition, no teacher, however sincere, is considered to be qualified to represent it if the requirements of 1) discipleship training, 2) practice to the level of Self-realization, and 3) empowerment (ordination and permission to teach given by one's guru) have not been met. Teachers who claim to have been instructed or empowered by a guru of this tradition who appeared in a vision or dream or who communicates advice or guidance by mental telepathy, are not to be believed.

The first publicly known guru in this lineage is a fully enlightened saint known as Babaji. Because he prefers to have personal contact with only a few carefully chosen disciples, information regarding his life and activities is scarce. By using little known methods of physical regeneration and the power of his illumined consciousness, Babaji has maintained a youthful physical body for centuries. Although his abode is in the seclusion of the Himalayan mountains, his awareness is not confined to this realm or limited by space or time.

In the mid-1800s, during the dawning of the current era of global spiritual awakening, having revived the ancient kriya yoga methods which had become obscured with the passage of time, Babaji chose to make them available to sincere truth seekers in all walks of life.

In 1861, Shyamacharan Lahiri, then thirty-three years of age, who lived with his wife in Banaras, India, and was employed as a clerk for the British military road building department, traveled on a work assignment to the Nainital District in the foothills of the Himalayas. There, on Drongiri Mountain near Ranikhet, he met a man who took him to the entrance of a cave dwelling, where Babaji awaited them. Babaji welcomed Lahiri and touched his spiritual eye to activate his memories of their guru-disciple relationship which had been established in a previous incarnation.

Within two weeks, after being instructed in a variety of meditation practices, Lahiri acquired the ability to experience transcendent, superconscious states of awareness. Before departing to return to his family and work duties, Lahiri requested permission to instruct and initiate others. After discussing the matter for some time, Babaji said, "When they are prepared, teach kriya practices to all who sincerely ask for help on the spiritual path. Those whom you initiate must be honest and truthful."

Until his transition from the body in 1895, Lahiri fulfilled family and secular obligations and initiated more than five thousand men and women. He also wrote twenty-seven books of commentary on various scriptures. His disciples reverently referred to him as Lahiri *Mahasaya*, "one who is large-minded or cosmic conscious." Because he chose not to have his mission widely publicized, it was said of him that he was a "secret" yogi. When initiating a person he would advise, "Don't tell anyone about this matter. Live a good life and practice kriya meditation every day in the privacy of your home."

Of the several disciples of Lahiri Mahasaya who also initiated truth seekers, Swami Sri Yukteswar is most widely known. When he was born, he was given the name Priya Nath Karar. In his young adult years, he married, helped his mother manage the family-owned rental properties inherited from his father, and attended college classes for a brief period of time to learn anatomy and physiology. After his wife died following the birth of a daughter, he traveled extensively to acquire knowledge of Ayurveda, vedic astrology, and yoga practices. While visiting the city of Banaras (Varanasi), he became a disciple of Lahiri Mahasaya. Approximately ten years later, by then proficient in meditation, he began to initiate others. Years later, he was initiated into the swami order. The meaning of his monastic name *Yukteswar* ("one who is united with God") is derived from the Sanskrit words *yuj*, union, and *Iswara*, lord or ruler: the aspect of God that regulates the cosmic order.

In 1894, at a large, periodic gathering of saints and lay persons in Allahabad, India, Sri Yukteswar met Babaji who asked him to write a small book emphasizing universal truths. Within a short period of time the book, *The Holy Science*, was published. The introduction to the text provides a concise explanation of the esoteric influences which contribute to the cyclic increase and diminishment of spiritual awareness of the planet's human inhabitants.

Sri Yukteswar established two modest spiritual training centers, in Serampore near Calcutta and at Puri near the Bay of Bengal. He also founded meditation groups in several small villages and occasionally arranged public meetings to promote understanding and harmony among people of various faiths. One of his young disciples, Mukunda Lal Ghosh, whom he taught and trained with special care, was to become known throughout the world as Paramahansa Yogananda.

Born January 5, 1893, Paramahansa Yogananda's parents were disciples of Lahiri Mahasaya and devout practitioners of kriya yoga. At an early age he sought the company of saints and sages. He was first instructed in meditation practices by his father. After graduating from high school he met Sri Yukteswar in Banaras and was accepted for discipleship training. When, a few years later, Sri Yukteswar ordained him as a swami, he chose the monastic name *Yogananda*, "yoga [oneness with God]-bliss."

After ten years of intensive yoga training with Sri Yukteswar, Paramahansaji was invited to visit America, to speak at a Congress of Religious Liberals in Boston, Massachusetts. Sri Yukteswar told him, "If you go now, all doors will be open to you." Accepting the invitation, in

1920 he traveled by boat to America, spoke at the Congress, remained in Boston for three years to teach classes, and made plans to embark on his mission of introducing kriya yoga philosophy and practices to interested people in the West.

With funds donated by his Boston disciples, an extensive lecture tour was scheduled. Starting in Carnegie Hall in New York City, Paramahansaji traveled to many of the major cities of the United States, speaking to thousands of people and offering a progressive series of classes. Decades later, referring to those years of travel, he said, "I knew that only a few among the thousands of people who attended my lectures and classes would remain faithful to their practices. I was planting positive seeds [ideas] in their minds that would eventually be helpful to them. I was also preparing the foundation for the work that was yet to unfold."

During Paramahansaji's first visit to Los Angeles, in 1925, more than three thousand people attended his lectures. A hotel building and several acres of land in the Highland Park district of the city was purchased as the site for the international headquarters of his organization, which he named Self-Realization Fellowship. There, accommodations were provided for disciples who wanted to live with him in an ashram environment and volunteer their services to maintain and expand the growing work.

In 1946, my guru's book *Autobiography of a Yogi* (now distributed in nineteen languages) was published. A few years later, when asked why so many people declared that reading it had transformed their lives, he quietly said, "Because my spirit is in it."

During the last two years of his earth-life, except for occasional trips to Los Angeles, Paramahansaji remained in seclusion at his retreat house near Twentynine Palms, California. He completed the writing of his comprehensive commentary on the Bhagavad Gita, was accessible to a few disciples, and gave specific instructions to his appointed successors to assure the continuation of his work far into the future. He consciously left his body on March 7, 1952.

By earnest endeavor and God's grace, when I was eighteen years of age I met Paramahansa Yogananda and became his disciple. As a child I was self-motivated to discover the practical means by which my desire to know the purpose of my life and my relationship to God could be most quickly and efficiently fulfilled. While in high school, I read a book obtained from a public library that introduced me to the philosophy and practices of yoga. I then responded to a magazine advertisement which featured *Autobiography of a Yogi*. While avidly reading that book, I knew that the kriya yoga path was my own. In late December, 1949, I traveled to California and went to the Self-Realization Fellowship headquarters two days before Christmas, early in the evening. While being interviewed by a senior member of the monastic order, Paramahansaji entered the room. After greeting me, his first words were, "How old are you?" A few moments later he touched my forehead with his hand. "I'll see you again," he said, as he walked to the porch where his car awaited him.

Two days later, during our first private talk, my guru told me, "You should know that this [kriya yoga] path is not one of escapism." I was to learn that the purpose of spiritual practice is not to withdraw from the world. A kriya yogi must learn to always be superconscious while relating to others, skillfully performing ordinary duties, and living effectively with meaningful purpose.

When I was with my guru, he demonstrated by his presence and demeanor how a Self-realized person lives. He provided wise counsel and encouragement, freely shared his knowledge, and initiated and instructed me in spiritual practices. One evening in late autumn of 1951, a few months before he left his body, he transmitted to me the enlivening power of his enlightened consciousness and ordained me to teach. The essence of what I learned during those early years, and have personally realized during the decades that have passed since then, I now offer to sincere devotees on the spiritual path in this concise lesson format.

HOW KRIYA YOGA IS LEARNED

After being instructed in the basic philosophical concepts, lifestyle guidelines, and meditation routines, one acquires direct knowledge of what has been taught by attentive, sustained practice that provides opportunities for personal experience. Although the information about kriya yoga which has been promulgated during the past one hundred years has inspired many people, the best way to learn the principles and procedures and apply them effectively is to have the personal guidance and wise counsel of a competent teacher. Such a teacher of kriya yoga is one who has experienced its processes, whose spiritual forces are fully aroused, and who is Self-realized.

For the teacher-student (guru-disciple) relationship to be worthy of the teacher's time and attention and of benefit to the student, one who desires personal instruction and assistance on the spiritual path should have the following qualifications:

• Be sincere (honest, unpretentious, and dedicated).
• Have a wholesome, constructive lifestyle.
• Have respect for the tradition and the teacher.
• Be willing to learn and to practice what is learned.
• Have the intellectual capacity to learn and the functional ability to apply what is learned.

Sincerity and humility (complete absence of egotism) are essential if a person is to be receptive to learning. Egotism, often dramatized as arrogant self-righteousness reinforced by mental perversity, is a common characteristic of individuals who, because they are insecure and provincial (small-minded), are inclined to resist new ideas even if information freely provided to them is for their benefit.

A wholesome, constructive lifestyle that nurtures total well-being and supportive personal circumstances provides a firm basis for the cultivation of spiritual awareness.

If an individual does not respect the spiritual tradition through which life-transforming information is transmitted or the teacher who imparts it, learning cannot be experienced.

Receptivity to learning and diligent practice of what is learned will definitely result in satisfactory progress.

If one does not yet have the intellectual capacity to comprehend what is taught, misunderstanding will result. Intellectual powers should be developed and improved. Conditions which restrict one's ability to function effectively (a physical limitation, a learning disability, a severely imbalanced mind-body constitution, habitual neurotic behavior, addictive behaviors, psychotic episodes, or other conditions which interfere with sincere desire to accomplish purposes) should, whenever possible, be corrected.

If a physical limitation or learning disability cannot be entirely overcome, teaching methods and spiritual practice routines can often be adapted to the needs of the sincere truth seeker. Obsessive neurotic or addictive behaviors or disabling psychotic episodes, however, are major obstacles to learning and spiritual practice. Individuals who have these problems should not be involved with metaphysical studies or meditation practices until they have been restored to a functional level of psychological health. Neurotic or addictive tendencies which are only mildly troublesome can often be renounced by conscious choice and by practicing meditation daily to the stage of deep physical relaxation and mental peacefulness.

THE BASIC PRACTICES AND GUIDELINES

Kriya yoga practice is not for the superficially interested person who is merely curious; emotionally immature; inclined to indulge in fantasy; or addicted to mental attitudes, moods, or habitual behaviors which perpetuate illusions and delusions.

Illusions are inaccurate or mistaken perceptions of words, ideas, feelings, things, or circumstances. Illusions which are believed to be true are *delusions*.

It should be clearly understood that, for optimum benefits to be experienced by study and practice of these principles, one must be disciplined in the practical application of what is learned, and fully committed to the nurturing and actualization of authentic spiritual growth. Spiritual growth is authentic or real when the effects of its transformative influences are evident in our lives. The results of attentive study and diligent, right practice are:

· Enhanced intellectual and intuitive powers.
· Psychological transformation.

- Improved functional abilities.
- Orderly unfoldments of innate knowledge.
- Mental illumination.
- Progressive clarification of awareness.
- Spontaneous emergence of cosmic conscious states.
- Self-realization.
- God-realization.
- Liberation of soul awareness.

The novice kriya yoga student should first become familiar with the philosophical concepts and the lifestyle regimens (and their purposes) upon which practice is based. Knowledge of beginning, intermediate, and advanced meditation practices and routines should then be acquired. It should be understood that although knowledge and practice of meditation methods is important, everything that is done to nurture total well-being and to live effectively is of equal importance. At each stage of progressive awakening to authentic Self- and God-knowledge, the devotee's new state of awareness must be harmoniously integrated with the mind, personality, and body. This process is most effectively accomplished by appropriate, conscious living every moment of each day.

As skillful living becomes spontaneous, and proficiency in meditation practice improves, a sequential series of advanced meditation techniques can be learned. When these have been effectively practiced for a period of time and one is fully prepared, initiation, and instruction in more intensive meditation practices may be requested.

For soul-satisfying results, unwavering aspiration to spiritual growth balanced by calmness and patience is recommended. Aspiration that is allowed to fluctuate does not sustain enthusiasm or motivation. Impulsiveness often results in restlessness and feelings of despair.

Superior to the senses is the mind; superior to the mind is the intellect;
superior to the intellect is the Self [the essence of one's being].
– *Bhagavad Gita 3:42*

LESSON ONE / PART TWO

LIFESTYLE GUIDELINES

DISCOVER THE PURPOSE OF YOUR LIFE

> We are on earth but a little while. The real reason for being here is very different from what most people imagine. There is a fundamental purpose for our lives. To know it, we must know life's origin and where it is going, look beyond our short-term goals to what we ultimately want to accomplish, and consider life's highest potential for development.
>
> *– Paramahansa Yogananda*

For most people, life is experienced as a series of semiconscious dream episodes. Their feelings, desires, urges, thoughts, sensations, memories, and perceptions of events and circumstances are mixed together and constantly changing. Awareness is blurred and fragmented. Confused, they strive to fulfill their hopes and dreams, satisfy cravings, and experience interludes of enjoyment, satisfaction and disappointment. They become tired, old or disabled, and die with feelings of sadness and regret without ever having experienced real happiness. They are normal, conformed to the ordinary human condition. They do not always consciously intend to waste their lives. They do so because they do not know better, cannot do better, or have not wanted to expand their awareness beyond the boundaries of habitual modes of thinking.

ASK: "WHAT IS LIFE FOR?"

Think about it. Be curious. Use your common sense. Seek out sources of valid (well-grounded, reliable) knowledge. Apply yourself to learning. Inquire into the depths of your being where all knowledge resides. Investigate and experiment until you discover the answer.

For thousands of years, saints and sages have clearly defined the real purpose of life and the practical means by which permanent well-being, happiness, and spiritual fulfillment can be experienced. This is what they have said:

1. Learn to live in accord with the fundamental principles (laws) of nature which determine its actions and processes. Be on friendly terms with nature and all aspects of life. Attune your mind and awareness and conform your thoughts and actions to the inclinations and impulses of the intelligently directed Power that nurtures the universe. Choose to live wisely, simply, naturally, wholesomely, and constructively. Discover the role you are to play in the drama of life and play it well. Develop and skillfully use your knowledge, talents, and abilities to maintain your well-being and to assist others to their highest good.

This is the way of right (dharmic) living. *Dharma* is 1) the inherent urge or influence of Consciousness in relationship to creation that upholds and maintains its processes; 2) a life-path which is most compatible with one's temperament and abilities and which allows one to always be in harmonious accord with supportive influences. All of one's actions are then constructive and have beneficial effects, and personal fulfillment and spiritual growth are more easily experienced.

2. <u>Learn to have your life-enhancing desires easily fulfilled</u>. Desire to experience total health, well-being, harmonious relationships, the accomplishment of meaningful purposes, and rapid spiritual growth is natural and wholesome. All other desires should be renounced. Desires are impelling: they stimulate imagination and provide motivation to perform actions which will result in their fulfillment. Because your mind is a particularized aspect of the omnipresent Universal or Cosmic Mind, clearly defined desires, whether below the threshold of conscious awareness or consciously nurtured, tend to attract the necessary resources, events and circumstances which will enable them to be actualized.

Swami Sri Yukteswar said to Paramahansa Yogananda, "If the object of one's clearly defined desire does not yet exist, the universe will produce it for the person who desires it."

3. <u>Learn to have all of your real needs effortlessly satisfied</u>. When you are established in awareness of wholeness, know that you are an individualized aspect of one, all-pervading Consciousness. Live in accord with its processes and the actions and essences of nature and the impulses of God's grace will spontaneously provide the resources and supportive events and relationships that you need.

4. <u>Awaken to Self- and God-realization in this incarnation.</u> Dharmic living, easy fulfillment of desires which enhance life, and always being in a continuous flow of resources and supportive circumstances will enable you to live efficiently and avoid suffering and misfortune. To fulfill your soul destiny, avidly aspire to awaken to complete Self- and God-Realization—the primary purpose for your being in this world—and wholeheartedly engage in practices which will enable you to do so as quickly as possible.

Affirm With Soul-Aware Conviction
I am thankful for the understanding that I now have.
I am wholeheartedly dedicated to living a God-centered life.
I do my best to have my life-enhancing desires easily fulfilled
in cooperation with the natural laws of causation.
I am receptive to the impulses of grace and thankfully accept
the full support of the universe.
I intend to be fully Self- and God-realized in this incarnation.

LESSON ONE / PART THREE

MEDITATION PRACTICE

UNDERSTANDING AND USING MANTRAS

Words are symbols used to convey the reality and meaning of that which they define. By conscious, devotional utterance, intonation, and chanting of a sacred word [mantra] a divine vibration is awakened within our being. – *Lahiri Mahasaya*

mantra Word origin: *manas*, mind; *tra*, to protect, to take beyond.

A meditation mantra is a word, word-phrase, or sound used as a focus of attention to remove awareness from thoughts and feelings to allow the meditator's concentrated attention to be undisturbed. It is used only as long as needed; when attention is turned inward and meditation flows smoothly, it is disregarded. Several meditation mantras will be described in this section of the lesson.

Meditation is easy to learn and practice. The procedure has nothing in common with self-hypnosis, autosuggestion methods, or endeavors to produce mental phenomena or pleasant moods to comfort the mind or create a false sense of reality. Meditation is practiced by withdrawing attention from environmental conditions, physical sensations, emotions, and mental processes so that one's essence of being can be clearly apprehended and experienced.

Prevailing, disordered fluctuations (movements and changes) of thoughts and moods distort, modify, and confine soul awareness and blur the intellect. Even though the pure-conscious nature of the soul remains ever the same, it is not easily experienced when attention is overly involved with mental processes and emotional states. For meditation practice to be effective, the meditator must remain alert and attentive while quieting restless thoughts and emotions that obscure the soul's perception of its real nature.

The final result of effective meditation practice is described in the second verse of the first chapter of Patanjali's *yoga-sutras* (1:2):

Yoga [transcendent superconsciousness] is realized when fluctuations in the individualized field of awareness cease [because of having restrained and restored to their origins].

Mental and emotional states are easily restrained and pacified when they are ignored and the meditator's attention is directed to the object that has been chosen as a focus of concentration.

Mastery of attention is the key to consciously experiencing Self- and God-awareness. If one is not alert when thoughts and emotions subside, if attention is diffused or if apathy (indifference) is habitual, the ordinary self-conscious (egocentric) state will tend to prevail or the meditator may drift into a state of passive reverie or sleep.

The mere absence of awareness of thoughts and moods does not always result in enhanced soul awareness and God-knowledge. If it did, everyone would be enlightened because of observing regular episodes of sleep and occasionally being distracted from their thoughts and feelings while in the waking state.

By remaining alert when thoughts and emotions subside, a shift of viewpoint from ordinary self-consciousness to superconsciousness can spontaneously occur. To calm mental and emotional restlessness, a balanced, twofold approach is recommended: right living and alert practice of superconscious meditation.

A *super*conscious (over, above, transcendent) state is other than, independent, and superior to ordinary waking states, subconscious, and unconscious states. Aspire to experience superconsciousness, to go beyond mental and emotional states to clear, tranquil awareness. Rest there for a while, then aspire to experience more refined states.

The progressive unfoldments of superconsciousness:

1. <u>Superconscious awareness mixed with thoughts and emotions</u>. At this stage of practice, the meditator is poised, emotions are calm, and thoughts are not forceful. The Self-aware meditator, observing mild mood changes and subtle thought processes, may question whether or not a superconscious state is being experienced. Repeated episodes of this kind cause constructive psychological changes, clarify awareness, inspire the meditator to persist, confirm the usefulness of the experience, and banish doubts.

2. <u>Free-flowing superconscious awareness</u>. Attention flows to the meditative object or ideal without interruption. Secular concerns, physical sensations, emotional states, memories, and thoughts are disregarded. This is the stage of effortless, meditative contemplation.

3. <u>Absorbed superconscious awareness</u>. Contemplation culminates in identification of awareness with the meditative object or ideal: inner sound (Om), light, joy, or space (formlessness). Awareness is so absorbed that, after meditation, one remembers, "I was sound, light, joy, space (or whatever was vividly perceived)." This stage, while extremely beneficial because it sustains superconsciousness which constructively impacts and purifies the mind, should eventually be transcended because it is not yet the ultimate stage to be realized. It is "superconsciousness supported by that which is perceived."

4. <u>Refined superconscious awareness</u>. As awareness is clarified, the mind is increasingly illumined and psychological transformation occurs. Cosmic consciousness (intuitive apprehension of the seamless wholeness of life) unfolds. The reality of Consciousness beyond the

boundaries of space and time, and the intelligence-directed power of Consciousness from which the universe is produced and by which it is sustained, is intuitively apprehended.

5. <u>Transcendent superconscious awareness devoid of attributes or characteristics</u>. Pure realization of absolute Existence-Being which is not supported by an object of perception. When this realization is permanent, awareness is liberated from all conditions which formerly modified and confined it.

HOW TO PRACTICE MEDITATION FOR PERSONAL BENEFITS AND AUTHENTIC SPIRITUAL GROWTH

For superior results, meditate on a regular, daily schedule in a quiet place where you will not be disturbed. Early morning, before starting your ordinary activities, is an ideal time. If early morning is not suitable because of a work schedule, family obligations, or because you are not alert after waking from sleep, any other time can be chosen. By adhering to a daily practice schedule, you will soon become proficient and have satisfying results.

Although the primary purpose of meditation practice should be to nurture spiritual growth, several side-benefits will result:

· Reduction of stress because of deep, physical relaxation.
· Ordering and calming of mental processes and emotions.
· Strengthening of the body's immune system.
· Slowing of biologic aging processes.
· Functional improvement of the body's organs and systems.
· Alertness and higher energy levels.
· Improved powers of concentration and of intellectual ability.
· Easier overcoming or renouncing of addictive tendencies.
· Enhanced appreciation and enjoyment of life.

Approach each practice session with optimism. If you are a new meditator, be patient. Practice the methods and routines in the order described in these lessons. Acquire a comfortable degree of skill at each level before proceeding to the next level.

The easiest way to learn to meditate is to use a mantra: a word, word-phrase, or sound to which your attention is naturally attracted. For beginning meditators who are primarily interested in eliciting the side-benefits described above, the words *peace*, *joy*, *happiness*, or any pleasant word may be used. An adherent of Judaism might prefer the Hebrew *shalom*, a Hindu might prefer the Sanskrit *shanti*—words which mean *peace*. *God* (in any language) or *Om* may also be used.

Examples of word-phrase mantras are *Om-God* and the commonly used Sanskrit mantras *hong-sau* and *so-hum*. *Om* is the sound current-vibration of the all-pervading power of Consciousness.

When one word is used, it is mentally recited when inhaling or when exhaling. As attention becomes internalized, the word is mentally "listened to" instead of mentally recited.

The constructive, vibrational influences of the mantras *hong-sau* (pronounced hong-saw) and *so-hum* enliven the nervous system, reduce stress, and introduce calming, transformative influences into the mind and body.

When using a word-phrase, the first word is mentally recited with inhalation; the second word is mentally recited with exhalation. As attention becomes internalized, the words are mentally "heard" rather than mentally recited. *Listening* is a refined form of practice that takes the meditator's attention inward to more subtle levels of mind and awareness. If you have been given a mantra by a qualified teacher and it works for you, use it.

Meditate this easy, natural way:

• Sit upright, in a comfortable chair. If a cross-legged sitting posture is more comfortable for you, sit like that.

• It can be helpful to acknowledge your relationship to the Infinite. If you want to pray to become aware of God's presence, do so. If you are an initiated disciple of an enlightenment path, acknowledge the teachers and saints of your tradition. Let their prayers on your behalf and your reverent respect for them inspire you as you meditate.

• Poised and alert, direct your attention to the spiritual eye center between your eyebrows. It is not necessary to strain to do this; just have your awareness focused there.

• Observe your natural breathing rhythm. Let it flow easily. If using a one word mantra, mentally recite it when you breathe in; feel peaceful when you breathe out. (Optional: recite the mantra only when you exhale. Experiment until you discover which method produces the most favorable results.) With a word-phrase mantra, mentally recite the first word when you inhale; recite the second word when you exhale. With either mantra, as you become more internalized, mentally listen to the mantra rather than recite it.

• When you are relaxed and internalized, disregard the mantra and rest in that calm, alert state for the duration of the session.

• To conclude your practice: open your eyes, remain calmly poised for a few moments, then resume your normal activities.

Be attentive to the mantra until you no longer need it. As you become more relaxed, notice that your breathing becomes slower and less forceful and your thoughts are calm and orderly. If you become distracted from the mantra, return your attention to it. If your attention is distracted or you become too passive while meditating after using the mantra, choose to be more alert.

Avoid preoccupation with memories, moods, thoughts, or mental visions which may be produced by the restless mind when your eyes are closed. If such distractions persist, open your eyes, gaze straight ahead without focusing on anything, and continue to meditate. When you are again alert, close your eyes and look into the spiritual eye.

Maintain a poised, upright posture. Avoid allowing your head to drop downward, as this may cause you to drift into a passive, semiconscious state, or sleep. If sleepiness or tiredness is an obstacle to meditation practice, schedule more time for regular hours of sleep and review your nutrition and exercise program to ensure that you always have a high level of energy. Other obstacles which may have to be overcome are described in the *yoga-sutras* (1:29,30):

> By attentive practice of meditation on God, all obstacles are removed. [Some] obstacles to the accomplishment of samadhi [realization of wholeness] are illness, doubt, negligence, philosophical confusion, lack of progress, instability, addiction to sense perceptions, misperceptions, and mental distractions.

If you are a new meditator, start by practicing for twenty minutes once or twice a day. This will allow ample time for relaxation and inner peace to be experienced. It is more useful to meditate with alert attention for twenty minutes than to meditate for a longer period of time in a passive state.

Avoid anxiety about the outcome of meditation practice. Include it in your daily routine and live a wholesome, purposeful life. Benefits will soon be obvious.

It can be helpful to set aside a private place for deep meditation and communion with the Infinite. Have a comfortable chair, or a mat if you sit on the floor. You may also want to have an altar, with pictures of saints or other items of symbolic value, and special books from which you derive information and inspiration. When you are there, disregard all mundane matters and personal problems. Concentrate only on your purpose: to be mentally refreshed and spiritually conscious.

Meditate in silence. Some novice meditators try to meditate while listening to soothing music that elicits a pleasant mood. Even though they may experience a degree of relaxation, they cannot experience a meaningful superconscious state. Listening to inspirational music prior to meditation practice, or at any other time, is a matter of personal preference. For superior results when meditating, choose a silent environment, withdraw your attention from the senses, and abide in the sanctuary of the soul.

To enrich your practice, once each week, every two weeks, or once each month, meditate twice as long as you usually do. Doing this will provide you with the opportunity to go more deeply within. However, do not become so preoccupied with subjective meditation perceptions that you neglect your duties and responsibilities. Live a balanced life.

When you first sit to meditate, if you are not inspired:

• Pray to arouse your soul forces: audibly at first if you are inclined to do so, then silently. If you prefer not to pray, aspire to realize (apprehend and experience) your true nature and the reality of the wholeness of Consciousness.

• Remind yourself of the value of meditation practice and of your resolve to fully awaken and actualize your innate potential.

Adhere to your chosen meditation schedule as a spiritual duty. Physical or mental restlessness and subconscious resistance to practice will weaken and subside as meditative calmness begins to prevail and superconscious states emerge.

Don't rely on others to support your resolve to acquire higher knowledge and to be attentive to spiritual practice. If you have such support, be thankful. If you do not have it, summon the strength you need from within yourself. Be Self-inspired and highly Self-motivated. Learn to live skillfully and to meditate effectively. When you meditate, you are alone with God.

If you do occasionally meditate with your spouse or one or more friends, it is all right for one whose practice session is first concluded to quietly depart the meditation chamber.

The spiritual path is one of inward aloneness (not loneliness). The few years allotted by natural law for physical incarnation pass quickly. What are you doing to fulfill the real purpose of life? Make wise choices and immediately implement effective actions which will enable you to fulfill your soul destiny while you are in this world.

It is best not to talk with anyone except your spiritual teacher or a qualified professional counselor about your personal life, private studies, or spiritual practices. Be so inwardly strong that you never feel emotionally dependent. Whenever possible, avoid having to listen to erroneous opinions. Only an insightful person can comprehend the contents of your mind and the aspiration of the heart (soul).

He that dwells in the secret place of the most High
shall abide under the shadow of the Almighty.
– The Book of Psalms 91:1

REVIEW OF LESSON ONE

As you read these lessons, with a pen or pencil mark the themes which speak to you and write notes for your future use in the space beside the texts.

1. What are *kriyas*? _____

2. What is *yoga*? _____

3. How can rapid, authentic spiritual growth be nurtured?

    _____

4. What qualifications should a kriya yoga student have?

    _____

5. What are some of the results of attentive practice of kriya yoga?

    _____

6. What are the four primary aims of life to fulfill?

    _____

7. What is a meditation mantra? Why is it used?

    _____

8. What are the five progressive stages of unfoldment of superconscious states?

    _____

9. What are some of the constructive side-benefits of right meditation practice?

    _____

10. Write a clearly defined affirmation to declare your resolve to be attentive to a lifestyle that supports your aspiration to live effectively and unfold your spiritual potential.

    _____

    _____

PERSONAL APPLICATION

What is your calendar age? _____

Are you in good health [ ] yes [ ] no
If not, what will you do to be restored to good health?

_____

Do you have any functional disabilities that need to be corrected? [ ] yes [ ] no
If you do, what will you do to correct them?

_____

Are your personal relationships harmonious and supportive? [ ] yes [ ] no
If not, what will you do to improve them?

_____

Is your work, occupation, or profession enjoyable to you? [ ] yes [ ] no
Does it provide a real service? [ ] yes [ ] no
If not, either learn to enjoyably perform it skillfully or consider doing something else. If what you do does not provide a real service for the benefit of others or harms the environment, do something that will benefit others and the environment. Offer all of your thoughts, actions, and the results of your actions to God and the universe.

How many more years do you expect to live in this incarnation? _____
Focus your attention and actions on essential matters that will enable you to accomplish all of your meaningful purposes while you are here.

Have a life-plan. Decide how much time and attention to allot for self-improvement studies, spiritual practice, work or service, family or social interaction, recreation and self-care, and whatever else you consider to be important or of real value to you. By concentrating on what is essential and disregarding nonessential matters you will be able live more effectively, be healthier and happier, and accomplish purposes which are worthwhile.

Write a list of your priorities in the order of their importance.

1 _____ 2 _____ 3 _____

4 _____ 5 _____ 6 _____

7 _____ 8 _____ 9 _____

THE WISDOM OF SWAMI SRI YUKTESWAR

Only a few [individuals] can rise above the influence of their professed creeds and find absolute unanimity in the truths propagated by all great faiths. People who are wholly engrossed in mundane concerns are in need of help and guidance from those holy beings who bring light to humanity. All creatures, from the highest to the lowest, are eager to realize three things: existence, consciousness, and bliss.

Human beings have faith and believe intuitively in the existence of a Substance of which the objects of the senses—sound, touch, sight, taste, and smell, the component parts of this visible world—are but attributes. When identified with the material body, one is able to comprehend by the senses these attributes only, not That to which they belong. God, the only Substance in the universe, is therefore not comprehensible by the average person unless awareness is elevated above the attributes of nature.

When ideas relating to gross matters which are perceived in the waking state are compared with the ideas one has regarding one's dreams, the similarity that exists between them naturally leads one to conclude that the external world also is not what it appears to be. Looking further, one discovers that, when awake, all mental concepts are nothing but mere ideas resulting from the union of the objects of the senses with the sense organs. This process is effected by the mind and conceptualized by the faculty of intelligence.

When, even by the means of inference, the true nature of the manifest universe and the relation between it and one's essence of being is understood; and when it is understood that it is delusion [clouded, fragmented awareness] alone which causes souls to forget their true Self [soul] and experience suffering, one naturally wishes to be relieved from all misfortune. This liberation from the bondage of delusion becomes the primary aim of life.

Ignorance is erroneously believing what is not true. Because of ignorance, one is inclined to believe that the material world alone exists, to forget that this material realm is a mere play [manifestation of cosmic forces] occurring within the one field of supreme Consciousness.

Moral courage, when firmly established, removes all obstacles to salvation [liberation of consciousness]: hatred, shame, fear, grief, condemnation [of others], racial [or any kind of] prejudice, pride because of ancestry, and egotism [an exaggerated sense of self-importance sometimes dramatized as arrogance].

When rested by [kriya] pranayama practice, the nervous system is refreshed. If one daily rests the nervous system in this way, the physical body is vitalized. Life and death come under the control of the yogi who perseveres in the practice of pranayama.

By practicing [kriya] pranayama as advised by the guru, the sound of Om spontaneously manifests. Breathing then becomes regulated and physical aging is slowed.

LESSON TWO

PHILOSOPHY

GOD'S REALITY, LIFE, POWER, AND SUBSTANCE

God is without beginning or end, complete and eternal; the one, indivisible Being. – *Sri Yukteswar*

God A being thought of as the perfect, omnipotent, omniscient originator of the universe [and souls], the principle object of faith and veneration of [adherents of] monotheistic religions.

– *Webster's Dictionary*

What is God? Does anyone know God? If God *has* been known by some people, can God be known by everyone? If so, how can we most quickly apprehend the full reality of God? Does God actually have a name and a personality? Is God male or female—or both? Does God really love or care about humans, creatures, and global or cosmic conditions? The answers to these questions may not always be what one expects, or wants, to hear.

The word *god* is traced through Old English to Germanic and Indo-European languages in which a corresponding ancestor form means "the invoked one." The surviving related word is Sanskrit *hu*. In the *Rig-veda*, the oldest known religious scripture, *puru-hutas* (much invoked) is used to refer to Indra, the "god" (cosmic influence) then thought of as the ruler of rain and thunder. To *invoke* (from Latin *invocare*) is to call on or appeal to for support or inspiration

"God" is not the actual name of the transcendent Reality millions of people aspire to realize. Names for God are used to refer to or attempt to define or describe the one, supreme (Latin *superus*, upper, over) Consciousness which, although self-existent and beyond the boundaries of time, space, and relative circumstances, by its self-manifesting power emanates and pervades the phenomenal worlds.

Many Christians pray to God as a heavenly father whom they believe loves them, cares about their well-being, can protect them from harm, and has the capacity to provide healing, resources, and a variety of fortunate circumstances. They believe that if they live a good life and have faith, God will forgive their sins (errors of thinking and behavior) and grant them salvation.

In the Old Testament, the Israelites referred to Yahweh as "the God of our fathers." When Moses, who was educated in Egypt, asked for knowledge of God, the inner response to his inquiry was, "I am what I am." Elohim, a Hebrew name for God, can also signify a variety of gods or concepts of God people might have.

Muslims refer to "the creator of heaven and earth who alone can redeem souls and provide physical sustenance" as al-Lah, the one, absolute Reality. The aspect of divinity which is turned toward the world is referred to as The Face of God. In the Koran, the sacred book of the Islamic faith, ninety-nine names or attributes of God are mentioned, which devotees may reverently recite or chant as mantras to nurture devotion and awareness of the presence of God.

Hindus (adherents of *sanatana dharma,* the "eternal, righteous way") refer to Absolute or Supreme Consciousness as Brahman; the name given to its expansive aspect is Brahma. Many other names for God are often used to define and describe the aspects, attributes, and influential powers of Consciousness which make possible its self-manifestations, actions, and processes. Some of these names may also indicate the gender attributed to the gods and goddesses (cosmic forces). Causative, forceful, or controlling characteristics are considered masculine; characteristics related to manifestation and nurturing are considered feminine. Masculine characteristics are attributed to Brahma, which is expansive and emanates its forces; Vishnu, the influence which preserves and maintains what has been manifested; and Shiva, the influence which transforms. The creative energies of each aspect are designated as their feminine companions (wives) without which they would be powerless.

Statues of Ganesha, with an elephant's head, a large abdomen, and four hands are installed in many Hindu temples and placed on altars in the homes of devotees who acknowledge God as "the remover of all obstacles." Wisdom-knowledge is symbolized by the unique head. Ganesha's large abdomen is a reminder that everything is contained within God. One hand is raised in blessing, indicating "do not be afraid." Each of the other three hands holds an object. A sweet, pure food offering confers health and prosperity. A lotus flower represents the qualities of selflessness and purity of motive. A small hatchet represents the cutting away or removal of base desires and the illusional sense of selfhood which obscures awareness of one's true nature and relationship to God. Devout Hindus acknowledge one God. They do not worship idols; they revere *ideals.*

Monotheism, belief in one (*mono*) God (*theos*) is the fundamental doctrine of Christianity, Islam, Judaism, Hinduism, and some other religions. Within these are many subdivisions or sects, with teachings promulgated in accord with the philosophical ideas or preferred practices of their members. We need not be overly concerned about the diverse opinions and modes of behavior of people who do not share our views and preferences. The paths chosen by truth seekers in their endeavors to know God are in accord with the sincerity of their desire, psychological temperament, and capacity to learn and comprehend.

External forms of worship can often be helpful, as can visits to temples, shrines, and special places of pilgrimage which are known to be centers of spiritual (pure or refined) energies. The internal way to directly apprehend Self- and God-knowledge is that of intellectual examination of the facts of life and contemplative meditation. One who is Self- and God-realized may choose to continue to observe outer modes of ritual because of the enjoyment derived from participation or for the benefit of others. Anchored in the Infinite, the enlightened soul is not influenced by transitory events and circumstances which occur in the mundane realm.

THE PRACTICAL VALUE OF ACCURATELY DEFINING PHILOSOPHICAL CONCEPTS AND KNOWLEDGE OF CONSCIOUSNESS, ITS ASPECTS, AND PROCESSES

Perceive the truth of what you examine. Think rationally. Define your insights or concepts with accuracy. Be specific when you think and speak. Avoid vagueness and uncertainty.

In an attempt to create an impression of being open-minded, one who is not informed may say, "It doesn't matter which religion one chooses, they all teach the same things." Only a little investigation is needed to discover that not all religious doctrines and practices are the same.

Another example of irrational thinking is the statement, "God is love." When we love someone, we do not declare the object of our affection to be love, nor do we say that the person who loves us is love. We may say that we love God or describe our perception of the attracting influence of God as love. An object of attention and affection is not its definition or description.

Just as God is not our opinion of what God is, neither is God the attributes or characteristics of Consciousness.

• Supreme Consciousness is devoid of modifying attributes.
• The only outward self-expression of Supreme Consciousness is the Godhead or Oversoul with three modifying attributes. The three modifying attributes which regulate cosmic forces are 1) *Sattva guna* with the power of attraction; 2) its polar opposite, *tamas guna* with the power of repulsion; 3) *rajas guna* with transformative influence. These three attributes also pervade the realm of nature because the universe is emanated, manifested, and pervaded by God.

When the modifying attributes in the Godhead are not in a state of equilibrium and the influence of repulsion is dominant, the power of Consciousness is projected as a vibrating force (Om). The vibrating force of Consciousness produces within itself a field of Primordial Nature (space, time, and cosmic forces) which further manifests as a field of Universal Mind and subtle, astral, and physical realms. When causal, astral, and gross material essences have been fully expressed by the involutional processes of Primordial Nature, evolutional actions elicited by the attracting power of Consciousness are enlivened and a physical universe emerges. After billions of years, when galaxies, solar systems, and planets are formed, life emerges.

Interactions of the Spirit, the enlivening essence of the Godhead, with the projected, vibratory power result in the individualization of units of pure Consciousness, a process which continues to occur.

Souls relate to their environment in accord with their prevailing states of awareness: which may be Self-aware, somewhat occluded or blurred, confused, or unconsciously identified with the characteristics of Primordial Nature. Some souls, absorbed in God-conscious bliss, do not become identified with the gross characteristics of Primordial Nature. Confused or unconscious souls are inclined to be attracted to causal, astral, or physical realms with environmental conditions and circumstances which correspond to their states of awareness.

A few souls never become unaware of their true nature. Some souls, because only partially deluded, temporarily reside in a refined causal realm until they reawaken to Self-realization. Many souls, unconsciously impelled by the force of inertia, become identified with astral and physical realms and remain there until they awaken through the stages of spiritual growth and reclaim awareness of their original, clear state of being.

Absolute, pure Consciousness is referred to as the Supreme Self; a *unit* is referred to as an individualized Self, the true essence of being of every person and creature. An individualized Self with awareness blurred because of becoming identified with or influenced by the characteristics of Primordial Nature is referred as to a soul. It is the awareness-clouded soul that is in need of being redeemed by having its awareness clarified and restored to its original, pure state.

At the innermost level, the Self is changeless, pure, whole, and serene. Knowledge of Consciousness and its processes is innate to the Self; only at the surface of awareness can confusion and ignorance exist. Self-Realization is conscious recognition of the truth of Being. One who is Self-realized can easily apprehend and experience the reality of God. Until Self-realization is flawless and permanent, the faculty of purified intelligence and highly developed powers of intuition should be used to comprehend the reality of God and the facts of life. Having information about God and how to live does not liberate the soul; only realized knowledge is liberating.

It is most helpful to aspire to know the full reality of God rather than to be satisfied with partial knowledge. Many men and women whose divine qualities have been obvious, and who may be thought of as saints, have had occasional or frequent glimpses of the reality of God and have communed with God while retaining their illusional sense of independent selfhood apart from God. When the illusional sense of selfhood is purified, whether one is meditating or engaged in ordinary activities, perception of God's wholeness is complete.

Why did God create the universe? Why did God create souls? Why does God allow war, poverty, and suffering? When the reality of God is comprehended, such questions will not be asked. When the reality of God is not comprehended, there are no answers which will completely satisfy the mind of the person who asks them.

God did not create souls; souls are individualized units of pure Consciousness which became identified with Primordial Nature and its characteristics because of the influence of inertia. Consciousness, the true Self of everyone, is immortal.

Questions such as, "Why does God allow war, poverty, and suffering," arise only when God is imagined to be a cosmic person with thoughts and feelings similar to those which are characteristic of the human or conditioned state of consciousness. God is the Oversoul, the one Being of which all units of life are aspects. God's power and substance manifested and sustains the universe. The trends of evolution are inexorably driven by the transformative inclinations of Consciousness. Human conditions are, for the most part, the result of the individual and collective mental states, states of consciousness, and behaviors of the human inhabitants of the planet. Instead of asking why God allows misfortune, we should ask, "What should I be doing to assist myself to well-being and to help others be healthy, happy, secure, and spiritually aware?"

People who prefer to complain, and who implore God to intervene in human affairs while doing little or nothing to acquire higher knowledge or to develop and use their creative abilities, have chosen to remain emotionally immature. Meaningful solutions to their real or imagined problems will only be discovered when they decide to be responsible for their thoughts, states of consciousness, and actions.

Devotees who have an infantile (childish, undeveloped) mentality are inclined to have a dependent attitude in relationship to God. They want to be nurtured, cared for, and protected. They usually prefer to think of and relate to God as a substitute father or mother, or to hope that an avatar or messiah will appear on the world scene to do for them what they should be doing for themselves. If they are fortunate enough to have a relationship with a competent spiritual teacher, they tend to exaggerate the teacher's degree of realization or expect the teacher to solve their problems, lighten the burden of their karma, and guarantee their enlightenment and salvation. To them, delusions and fantasies are more appealing than truth. Their real need is to be healed of their ignorance, which can only occur when they are willing to grow to emotional maturity, acquire valid knowledge, and help themselves to wholeness.

The philosophical concept of avatars, unique incarnations of divine qualities which periodically occur to vitalize evolutionary processes, is widely misunderstood. The idealized belief is that avatars are actual physical embodiments of God with flawless knowledge and unlimited powers and abilities. Through the centuries there have been many men and women whose obvious spirituality, wisdom, and selfless good works continue to benefit and inspire us. A dispassionate examination of their lives, however, is revealing. Like most people (but unlike God) they, too, had obstacles to overcome and were not always able to easily accomplish their purposes.

Many Self- and God-realized souls with exceptional knowledge and extraordinary abilities do live among us. The radiance of their spiritual enlightenment helps to clarify and beneficially transform the collective consciousness of the planet. While we can be thankful for their presence and their constructive influences, it is important for us to understand that, because God is equally incarnated as every soul, it is the spiritual awakening and enlightenment of all souls that allows God's transformative influences to be expressive.

HOW TO KNOW GOD

To know God, first know your Self. Acquire accurate information about God from reliable sources, adopt wholesome living regimens, meditate to clarify your awareness, and engage in Self-analysis. Ask: "What am I?" By using your common sense, powers of discriminative intelligence, and intuition, you will discover that you are not what you perceive as being other than you. You are not your body which had a beginning and will have an end. You are not the changeable personality. You are not the mind—the processes of which you observe. You are not what you may have imagined yourself to be or what others think you are. You are a whole, flawless, individualized aspect of one field of Consciousness. What you are, you have ever been and will ever be. At the core of your being you are enlightened. Comprehend this fact. Learn to unfold and actualize your innate knowledge and abilities.

Until you are Self-realized, it is all right to pray to God. Imagine any form or use any concept of God that is acceptable until you are able to comprehend what God is. Pray for understanding. Let your illusional sense of selfhood, the primary obstacle to awakening to God-realization, dissolve. You need not endeavor to attract God's attention. God is around you, within you, and individualized as you. Merge your awareness into the formless reality of God.

Pray *in* God. If you are asking God to respond to you, you are still thinking that God is separate from you. If you demand or insist that God answer your prayers or satisfy your desires or needs, your egotism, reinforced by arrogance, will perpetuate the illusion of separateness. Don't demand anything of God. Acknowledge, claim, and accept what is already available to you in God's wholeness.

> Ask, and it shall be given to you; seek, and you shall find;
> knock, and it shall be opened to you.
> – *New Testament / Matthew 7:7*

LIFESTYLE GUIDELINES

LIVE IN TUNE WITH THE INFINITE

The laws of life can teach us to live in harmony with nature and all aspects of life. When we know what the laws are, and conduct ourselves in accord with them, we experience lasting happiness, good health, and perfect harmony.

– Paramahansa Yogananda

ayurveda I-yur-ved-ah. *Ayus*, life; *veda*, [revealed] knowledge.

The laws of life which determine how its processes occur can be understood by examining the relationships and interactions of relative phenomena when specific conditions exist. From God to the material realm, they ensure that all causes produce corresponding effects. Because the laws of life are universal, whenever an event or circumstance occurs, we can be certain of the existence of a corresponding cause.

When we know the causes of events and circumstances that we experience, we can determine our own fate: what will definitely happen in the near or distant future because of the mental and emotional states, states of consciousness, and actions we choose and allow to prevail. God's grace is also a natural law that restores order to disordered circumstances. The entire universe is pervaded by the impulses of grace which empower evolution and are supportive of all living things. Grace empowers and supports us when we are receptive and responsive to it.

You can live in tune with the Infinite by being aware of the Power that nurtures the universe, learning the laws by which its intelligently directed purposes are accomplished, and willingly cooperating with those laws.

LIVE WITH MEANINGFUL PURPOSE

• Do you enjoy living?
• Are you sincerely interested in learning how to live in tune with the Infinite and in unfolding your innate, spiritual potential?
• Are you using your knowledge and functional abilities as effectively as you can—or are you struggling to survive, adapting to the views and behaviors of others because it is convenient to do so, or merely passively existing?
• Is everything you do, including your work, profession, or service that you render of real value to you, to others, and the planet?

A healthy, long life, lived with conscious intention, is of value because it will provide you with opportunities to accomplish all of your purposes in your present incarnation. Because of fewer deaths in

Basic Mind-Body Constitution Self-Evaluation Chart

Mark the dominant (1 only) description typical of you when you are rested and functioning well.

Characteristic	Vata (air)	Pitta (fire)	Kapha (water)
1. Body	( ) Narrow hips, shoulders	( ) Moderate	( ) Broad hips, shoulders
2. Body weight	( ) Thin, tendons show	( ) Medium	( ) Heavy
3. Endurance, strength	( ) Low, poor	( ) Fair	( ) High, good
4. Skin condition	( ) Dry, rough, cool, dark	( ) Soft, fair, oily, delicate, pink to red	( ) Oily, pale, moist, white
5. Skin, aging	( ) Dry, flaky, wrinkles	( ) Freckles, moles, pigmentation	( ) Smooth, few wrinkles
6. Hair	( ) Dry	( ) Medium	( ) Oily
7. Hair color	( ) Dark brown to black	( ) Light blond, red, light brown	( ) Medium blond, medium to dark brown
8. Hair texture	( ) Curly, kinky	( ) Wavy, fine, soft	( ) Strait or wavy, thick
9. Appetite, digestion	( ) Erratic, heavy, stays thin	( ) Sharp hunger	( ) Moderate, mild hunger
10. Teeth	( ) Large, protruding, crooked	( ) Yellowish, moderate	( ) White, large, little decay
11. Eyes	( ) Small, black or brown	( ) Hazel, green, grey	( ) Large, blue or brown
12. Bowel movements	( ) Dry, hard, constipation	( ) soft, oily, loose	( ) Heavy, slow, thick
13. Sex urge	( ) Frequent	( ) Moderate	( ) Cyclical, infrequent
14. Physical activity	( ) Flighty, restless	( ) Aggressive, focused	( ) Calm, steady
15. Voice, speech	( ) High pitched, fast, vibrato dissonant, weeping	( ) Medium-pitched, sharp, laughing	( ) Low-pitched, melodious, slow, monotone
16. Taste preferences	( ) Oily, heavy, sweet, soupy, salty, sour	( ) Medium, light, sweet, warm, bitter, astringent	( ) Dry, light, low-fat, sweet, pungent
17. Emotional state	( ) Insecure, unpredictable	( ) Aggressive, irritable	( ) Calm, agreeable
18. Sleep pattern	( ) Short, insomnia	( ) Sound, medium	( ) Deep, easy, prolonged
19. Memory	( ) Short-term	( ) Good, but not prolonged	( ) Long-term
20. Financial behavior	( ) Spends quickly and unwisely	( ) Saves, though impulsive	( ) Saves and accumulates
21. When threatened	( ) Fearful, anxious	( ) Angry, irritable, fights	( ) Indifferent, withdraws
22. Dreams while asleep	( ) Fear, flying, running	( ) Fire, strife, emotional	( ) Of water, erotic
23. Mental tendencies	( ) Questions, theorizes	( ) Judgmental, artistic	( ) Stable, logical
24. Quality of pulse	( ) Thready, slithering	( ) Moderate, jumping	( ) Slow and graceful
25. Pulse beats	( ) 80–100 times a minute	( ) 70–80 times a minute	( ) 60–70 times a minute
	Subtotal Vata _____ **times 4 =** _____	**Subtotal Pitta** _____ **times 4 =** _____	**Subtotal Kapha** _____ **times 4 =** _____

The subtotals should add up to 100 percent. Write your basic mind-body constitutional type on page 46.

infancy and early childhood, better health services, the more widely known value of nutrition and self-care procedures, and acceptance of the idea that the normal span of human life can and should be 120 years or more, the number of people who are living to advanced ages while remaining healthy and productive is rapidly increasing. It is estimated that more than fifty thousand people in the United States are over 100 years of age, and that during the next few decades the centenarian population of the world will rapidly increase.

> *Before continuing with this lesson, use the chart on the facing page to determine your basic mind-body constitution.* You will then be able to choose behaviors and lifestyle regimens which are supportive of you and your aims and purposes in life. You will be healthier, more spiritually aware, more mentally competent, more emotionally calm and stable, more skillful in your interactions with the environment, and enabled to live with the full support of nature.

The basic mind-body constitution is determined by:

• The soul's karma (subconscious conditionings) and dominant state of awareness prior to conception.
• The mind-body constitution of the parents.
• The mental and emotional states of the mother.
• Other conditions in the mother's environment prior to giving birth.
• The planetary aspects which prevailed at the time of birth.

While learning and applying practical procedures for mind-body constitution balance, remember that spiritual awareness is the primary, determining factor. When spiritually awake, we are inclined to live constructively and do what is most beneficial. Then, when a challenge is presented, we will quickly act to restore order and balance to every aspect of our lives.

Deficiency of spiritual awareness can result in intellectual errors, mental confusion, irrational thinking, moodiness, emotionalism, and an unnatural, disorganized lifestyle. Any of the psychological states and behaviors which are common when awareness is clouded and the mind is conditioned by delusions, illusions, obsessions, memories of pain or failure, and habits which are life-suppressing rather than life-enhancing, might be present. These can contribute to discomfort, weaken the body's immune system, and unsettle the actions of the three doshas: the primary governing influences that determine the states of the mind-body constitution.

The most effective approach to total wellness is to choose a life-management program with thoughtful attention given to spiritual, psychological, and physical wellness, rather than concentrating on one aspect and paying little heed to the others. If spiritual awareness is cultivated and psychological and physical problems are ignored, results will usually be unsatisfactory. If we focus on physical routines while allowing mental and emotional states to be disruptive or our spiritual practices to be sporadic, we will not experience the total benefits we desire and deserve.

Three supportive matters to which to be attentive are food choices, sleep, and conservation and purposeful use of available energy. What we choose to eat, how we schedule our time so that sufficient rest is obtained to allow renewal, and whether or not we use our vital forces constructively, indicates our degree of self-esteem and commitment to healthy, meaningful living and spiritual growth.

To be healthy and functional, it is important that we have a clear sense of purpose for living and are resolved to that end. If we are not purposeful, if we do not know why we are living our lives, total commitment to healthy living routines will be difficult. Mental conflicts and emotional confusion that contribute to disinterested or erratic behaviors in everyday circumstances will also interfere with endeavors to actualize wholeness. Conscious selection of foods provides the opportunity to demonstrate willingness to be self-responsible for our well-being. Thoughtless or careless actions in one aspect of our lives indicate a tendency toward indifference and other self-defeating attitudes which may also be characteristic of how we routinely behave.

Regular, sound sleep rests the mind and renews the body. Many of the body's circadian rhythms (Latin, *circa*, about: *dies*, day)—the regular cycles of biological function, temperature, blood pressure, and hormone levels—can be disrupted because of irregular sleep patterns and lack of sleep. Some resulting life-suppressing effects may be tiredness, mental confusion, and impaired physical coordination. Sleep on a regular schedule in a dark, quiet place. Awaken refreshed and begin the day with alert, energetic, purposeful intention.

The Sanskrit word for conserving and constructively using vital forces is *brahmacharya* (divine-going). The ideal is to direct all inner forces to life-enhancing purposes and spiritual growth. When vital forces are dissipated mental powers are diminished, the body's immune system is weakened, and the doshas are unbalanced. Vital forces are dissipated by excesses of any kind: worry, anxiety, extreme effort to concentrate, restlessness, too much talking and laughing, overuse of any of the senses, ingestion of toxic substances, insufficient sleep or rest, too much socializing, and overwork. They are conserved by mental peace, emotional calmness, rational thinking, faith, moderate talking, prudent use of the senses, nourishing foods, sufficient sleep and rest, dispassion when interacting with others and the environment, relaxed accomplishment of purposes, meditation, and divine remembrance. Conserved vital forces are transmuted into subtle and fine essences to nourish the body and refine the brain and nervous system.

Some causes of discomfort or illness over which we have conscious control are: mental conflicts and psychological disturbances; excessive use of the senses and of the body; insufficient use of the senses and of the body; misuse of mental abilities, the senses, the body, and knowledge; and environmental factors.

We can learn by practice to be mentally calm, rational, and emotionally settled. We can manage stress and avoid exhausting the physical systems. We can learn to wisely use our senses. We can choose a sensible wellness program to strengthen and enliven the body. We can choose to use the knowledge we have and acquire more by study, observation, and experience. We can choose wholesome, supportive environmental conditions and learn to adapt to seasonal changes.

Even conditions which may have a genetic basis or which were caused by accidents can be addressed and often resolved. It is essential to understand that, as spiritual beings, we can implement intentional, causative influences which can change psychological, physical, and environmental circumstances. At the level of soul awareness there is nothing that needs to be healed. At this level we are ever serene and whole. Established in soul awareness, we can do practical things to cause desirable adjustments in the outer realm.

Cultivation of spiritual awareness is important because it impels thoughts and actions to be constructive, directly and beneficially influences the mind and body, and attracts supportive circumstances. Alert attention should also be directed to cultivating healthy psychological states and attending to the needs of the body. Preoccupation with psychological states and physical conditions, however, that results in self-centeredness is just as unwise as neglect. Perceive your mind for what it is: a creative medium with which to interact with outer and inner realities. Perceive your body for what it is: a vehicle through which to express and experience life. Avoid thinking of yourself as a mind or as a body; you are superior to both. Preoccupation with the body can lead to obsessive behaviors or to hypochondria (a persistent, neurotic belief that one is or is likely to become ill, often involving complaints which have no supporting causes).

We are psychologically healthy when we are growing steadily in the direction of emotional maturity. Every person born into the world must undergo progressive psychological transformations. When very young, we want to discover who we are—to have an identity. As we grow older, we attempt to be self-determined, to make our way in the world by self-reliant endeavors. Eventually, we desire to know our relationship with God. If our intellectual and emotional unfoldment is slowed or stopped, we may become victims of arrested growth. A major obstacle to spiritual growth and to helping ourselves to overall wellness is a mental attitude which is resistant to change, supported by unwillingness to help ourselves once valid knowledge of how to do so has been acquired. It is helpful to understand that, except in extreme instances of disability, we are primarily responsible for restoring ourselves to wellness if not yet completely well, and for remaining healthy and functional.

How Vata, Pitta, and Kapha doshas, the governing principles of biological and psychological processes, are produced.

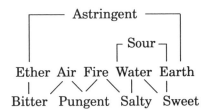

Field of Pure Consciousness
|
God: Oversoul
|
Primordial Nature
Om, space, time, cosmic forces
|
Universal Mind
Sattva   Rajas   Tamas
⁄＼   ｜ ＼ ⁄ ｜
Ether Air Fire Water Earth
 ｜ ⁄   ｜ ⁄   ＼ ｜
Vata   Pitta   Kapha
The governing principles
of biological functions.

Six Tastes Derived From the
Primary Element Influences

—— Astringent ——
┌── Sour ──┐
Ether Air Fire Water Earth
 ｜ ⁄ ＼⁄ ＼ ｜ ＼ ｜
Bitter Pungent Salty Sweet

Tastes which correspond to the element influences of the doshas (see above) increase them. Tastes which do not correspond to the element influences of the doshas decrease them.

THE ACTIONS OF THE THREE PRIMARY INFLUENCES ON THE MIND-BODY CONSTITUTION

The primary governing influences of the mind-body constitution are aspects of the five element essences, which are expressive aspects of the three constituents or attributes (gunas) of Consciousness which pervade the field of nature. Acquire an understanding of the actions of the gunas, element influences, and governing influences or doshas. Knowledge of these aspects of life and their roles in regulating mental and physical states will unfold from within your own consciousness.

When we are fully enlightened, we can remove ourselves from the influences of the doshas and the gunas. Until then, so long as we are identified with individualized existence and a mind or physical body, we have to cooperate with the influences which regulate nature's actions and processes.

Remember that doshas are subtle, influential forces. When their actions in our mind-body constitution are balanced, we experience psychological and physical wellness. When they are somewhat unbalanced, we may feel uneasy. When they are more obviously unbalanced—when one or more of the three dosha influences are excessive or deficient—discernible symptoms of unwellness can be observed and experienced.

Combinations of vata, pitta, and kapha influences are expressed in the psychological and physical characteristics of your basic mind-body constitution. When balance is maintained, health is optimum.

VATA DOSHA

Vata means "wind, to move, flow, direct the processes of, or command." It enables the other two doshas to be expressive. The actions of vata are drying, cooling, light, agitating, and moving. Vata sustains effort, inhalation and exhalation, circulation, impulses, tissue balance, and coordination of the senses. Its primary seat or location in the body is the colon. It also resides in the hips, thighs, ears, and bones, and is related to touch sensation. Vata, a combination of ether and air influences, is present and influential where there are spaces in which things (life force, thoughts, fluids, nerve impulses) move.

When vata dosha is disturbed or imbalanced, some symptoms can be anxiety, worry, a tendency to overexertion, insomnia, chronic tiredness, mental and emotional depression, physical tension and other symptoms of stress, a weakened immune system, headaches, underweight, constipation, skin dryness, erratic flows of life force and nerve impulses, mental confusion, emotional conflict, inability to make decisions, impulsiveness, fast and disconnected speech, fantasy, illusions, and sensations of being lightheaded and removed from thoughts, feelings, or circumstances.

Indications of balanced vata influences are mental alertness and abundance of creative energy, efficient elimination of waste matters, sound sleep, a strong immune system, enthusiasm, emotional balance, and orderly functioning of the body's systems.

People with a pronounced vata constitution or with a vata imbalance are advised to rest sufficiently, establish and maintain an orderly daily routine, and choose behaviors, personal relationships, foods, and environmental circumstances which can be instrumental in balancing vata characteristics. It is also important to regulate mental and physical impulses and to modify mental attitudes, emotional states, and behaviors in supportive ways.

Sweet, sour, and salty tastes decrease vata influences, so include these tastes if vata influences need to be diminished. Milk, wheat, rice, and some fruits and berries can provide sweet and sour tastes.

Regular exercise should be relaxed and moderate. Hatha yoga practice in a meditative mood is good, as are t'ai chi, walking, and swimming. Avoid strenuous, competitive, frantic activities.

When possible, associate with people who are calmly purposeful. Practice simple pranayama to calm the mind and balance flows of life force in the body. Meditate every day for deep relaxation.

PITTA DOSHA

Pitta (fire element essence) heats, digests, and is influential in chemical, biological, and psychological transformations. It is related to visual perception and the capacity to intellectually discern. A combination of fire and water element influences, it is present in the body in moisture and oils and in the fluids of the digestive system and blood. Pitta's primary seat or location in the body is the small intestine. It also resides in the eyes, stomach, sebaceous glands, blood, lymph, and perspiration.

When pitta influences are disturbed or out of balance, some symptoms can be excessive body heat, digestive problems, a tendency to be hostile or angry and controlling, impatience, a tendency to exert excessive effort to achieve goals, vision difficulties, and being prone to make errors in judgment because of mental confusion or because passion or emotion blurs powers of intellectual discernment.

Indications of balanced pitta influences are strong powers of digestion, vitality, decisive goal-setting inclinations, good problem-solving skills, keen powers of intelligence, boldness and courage, and a bright complexion.

People with a pronounced pitta constitution or a pitta dosha imbalance are advised to live more moderately, cultivate purity of intentions and actions, and choose foods, attitudes, behaviors, personal relationships, and environmental circumstances which can be instrumental in balancing pitta characteristics.

Because sweet, bitter, and astringent tastes decrease pitta influences, include these in your food plan if pitta characteristics are too pronounced. Complex carbohydrates, milk, and some fruits are sweet; some green, leafy vegetables are bitter; beans and some green vegetables are astringent.

Note: Food choices and lifestyle regimens can help restore and maintain the balance of the mind-body constitution. Select those which are in accord with your needs. Small portions of foods from the other lists can also be included. Use common sense. Avoid being obsessed in regard to foods and behaviors.

Foods and Lifestyle Regimens for a Vata Mind-Body Constitution:

Avoid dry, bitter tastes. Sweet, sour, and oily foods are helpful. Moderate use of dairy products if tolerated. Drink warm or hot water. Cinnamon, cumin, cardamom, ginger, cloves, and mustard are beneficial.

Vegetables	*Fruits*
cooked	sweet fruits
vegetables	apricot
asparagus	avocado
beets	bananas
carrots	berries
cucumber	cherries
green beans	coconut
onion, cooked	fresh figs
sweet potato	grapefruit
leafy green	grapes
vegetables	oranges
	melons
	peaches
	pineapple
	papaya

Grains: cooked oats, rice, wheat if tolerated.

Legumes: mung beans, black and red lentils, and tofu.

Oil: all are suitable.

Vata is aggravated during autumn and winter. Increase use of warm and oily foods during these seasons.

Do things that cool the mind, emotions, and body. Avoid conflicts and a tendency to be excessively competitive. Cultivate the virtues of honesty, morality, kindness, generosity, and self-control.

KAPHA DOSHA

A combination of water and earth influences, kapha is present in the body as moisture and dense substance. It holds things together. Mucus, for instance, indicates its influence. Kapha dosha provides nourishment, substance, support, and influences the body's tissues and lubricating aspects. Kapha psychological characteristics are modesty, patience, ability to endure, courage, a tendency to forgive, mental calmness, and emotional stability.

Kapha dosha effects are mostly cold, moist, heavy, and slow. In the blood and circulatory system, kapha influence is nourishing; pitta influence is energizing or heating; vata influence contributes to circulation. The balanced influences of the doshas result in good health and orderly functioning. The primary seat or location of kapha dosha in the body is the stomach. It also resides in lymph and fat. It is related to smell and taste sensation.

When kapha dosha influences are disturbed or out of balance, symptoms might be nausea, lethargy, a feeling of heaviness, chills, looseness of the limbs, coughing, mucus discharges, breathing difficulties, and a tendency to sleep too much. Other symptoms can be inertia, congestion, stagnation, and circulation problems. There may be a tendency toward obesity. Boredom, laziness, and mental dullness may be present.

Indications of balanced kapha influences are physical strength, a strong immune system, serenity, mental resolve, rational thinking, ability to conserve and wisely use personal resources and accumulate wealth, endurance, and adaptability.

People with a pronounced kapha constitution or a kapha dosha imbalance are advised to be receptive to useful change, renounce impediments to progress, be intentional in implementing life-enhancing actions, and choose foods, mental attitudes, behaviors, exercise routines, and relationships and environmental circumstances which can be instrumental in balancing kapha characteristics.

Pungent, bitter, and astringent tastes decrease kapha influences. Black pepper, ginger, cumin, chili, and some other spices provide the pungent taste; bitter is provided by some green, leafy vegetables; some green vegetables and beans provide the astringent taste. Note that the taste that decreases a dosha usually increases one or both of the other two. For general purposes, mildly increase the proportion of foods which are helpful while somewhat decreasing the proportions of others—having a sampling of all six tastes at your major meal.

Meditation can be more intensive for kapha constitutions than for vata or pitta types.

Foods and Lifestyle Regimens for a Pitta Mind-Body Constitution

Only moderate use of eggs, nuts, hot spices, honey, and hot drinks. Cool foods and liquids are better. Also sweet, bitter, and astringent tastes. Spices in moderation: black pepper, coriander, and cardamom.

Vegetables	*Fruits*
sweet and and bitter	sweet fruits
asparagus	apples
cabbage	avocado
cucumber	figs
cauliflower	dark grapes
celery	oranges
green beans	melons
leafy greens	mangos
mushrooms	pineapple
peas	prunes
green peppers	raisins
potatoes	
sprouts	
squash	

Grains: barley, cooked oats, basmati rice, wheat if tolerated.

Legumes: all except lentils. Dairy products in moderation if tolerated.

Oil: olive, sunflower, soy.

Pitta is aggravated during summer. Remain calm. Avoid excessive heat. Increase cooling foods and drinks.

The following quotations are from *Sushruta Samhita*, an ancient text on Ayurveda:

> One whose doshas are in balance, whose appetite is good, whose tissues are functioning normally, whose excretions are in balance, and whose physiology, mind, and senses are always full of bliss [the joy of life-awareness], is a healthy person.
>
> One should choose a livelihood [and lifestyle] with activities which are consistent with dharma [cosmic influences which uphold nature and society], adhere to the path of peace, and study to acquire knowledge. This is the way to happiness.

COOPERATING WITH DAILY AND SEASONAL RHYTHMS

Because dosha influences are determined by the three gunas which regulate cosmic forces, their characteristics expressive in our environment can influence our basic constitution. We can be healthy and functional by cooperating with daily and seasonal rhythms. Daily phases during which dosha influences prevail are as follows:

• Vata is influential from 2 a.m. to 6 a.m. (before sunrise). Awaken before 6 a.m. to eliminate body wastes and be attuned to the lightness and free flowing energy of vata dosha influences.
• Kapha is influential from 6 a.m. to 10 a.m. If possible, this is a suitable time to exercise because strength and stamina are at a peak level. It is also a good time to focus on work or activity that requires concentration and inner strength.
• Pitta is influential from 10 a.m. to 2 p.m. Because digestive fire is stronger during this phase, it is the ideal time to have the main meal of the day.
• Vata is influential from 2 p.m. to 6 p.m. Food and exercise should be light at this time of day.
• Kapha is influential from 6 p.m. to 10 p.m. To ensure adequate rest, go to sleep before 10 p.m.
• Pitta is influential from 10 p.m. to 2 a.m.

Adapt to the seasonal changes in your region of the world by relating to prevailing environmental conditions. Note these seasonal phases of dosha influences:

• Vata influences are pronounced during the winter months when the weather is cold and dry. At these times, maintain dietary and activity regimens which pacify or subdue mental and physical vata characteristics. Foods should be heavier and nourishing.
• Kapha influences are pronounced during the spring months when the weather is wet and moisture in nature replaces dryness. This is a good season of the year to implement a gentle body cleansing program and to observe dietary and activity regimens which pacify or subdue

Foods and Lifestyle Regimens for a Kapha Mind-Body Constitution

Avoid excessive use of sugar, salt, fats, and dairy products. Choose lighter foods. Avoid large quantities of food, cold drinks, and sweet, sour, salty tastes in excess.

Vegetables	Fruits
pungent	apples
& bitter	apricots
potatoes	berries
beets	cherries
broccoli	cranberries
cabbage	figs
carrots	peaches
cauliflower	mangos
celery	pears
eggplant	prunes
leafy greens	raisins
garlic	
onion	
peas	
peppers	

Grains: barley, corn, millet, oats, basmati rice in modest quantities.

Legumes: all except kidney beans and black lentils.

Oil: almond, corn, and sunflower in modest quantities.

Kapha dosha is aggravated during spring. Eat less, and add more dry, fibrous foods during this season.

kapha characteristics. Foods that increase pitta influences can be chosen. This is the time to implement a more active exercise program. Stay warm and dry. Cultivate warm emotional states.
• Pitta influences are pronounced during the summer months when the weather is hot. Maintain dietary and activity regimens which subdue pitta characteristics. Foods should be light and wet.
• During autumn, vata influences again prevail.

YOU CAN HELP YOURSELF TO TOTAL HEALTH AND FUNCTIONAL FREEDOM

As a spiritual being, you need not be a helpless effect of causes external to your essential (spiritual) nature. Avoid thinking that your mental states, emotional states, physical condition, personal relationships, or routine circumstances are solely the result of causes over which you have no control. It is unwise to think or say that you are unable to choose how to experience your life. Even though imbalanced dosha influences can contribute to mental and emotional confusion and physical unrest, they can be regulated by improved spiritual awareness, adjustments of mental and emotional states, and supportive lifestyle routines and behaviors. Whatever psychological or physiological characteristics you might presently be expressing, if they are not entirely life-enhancing, change them by choosing constructive behaviors.

Never affirm that you cannot help yourself to total wellness and functional freedom. At the core of your being, you are whole and free. Nurture spiritual growth. Read reliable philosophical literature—the writings of enlightened people. Meditate regularly until your awareness is established in superconscious tranquility, and learn to live with intentional purpose. Always be aware of the end results of your endeavors. Know why you do what you do. You will then more easily be self-motivated and goal-directed. You will be inspired to do whatever is necessary to be successful in your endeavors. When devoid of alert interest in life, without curiosity and drive, there may be a tendency to complacently drift, or to be uncaring and apathetic.

We were not born into this world to suffer, to continually cope with challenging conditions, or to struggle to survive. Suffering is due to lack of understanding and inappropriate living. We are here to learn about ourselves and the universe, unfold our innate soul abilities and capacities, live successfully, and be agents of divine purposes. The sooner we acknowledge why we are here and do what we can to enable ourselves to fulfill our purposes, the healthier and happier we will be.

Life-knowledge, when understood and correctly applied, enables us to effectively fulfill all of our mundane purposes and our spiritual destiny. Our mundane purposes are related to the realm of nature. They are the duties and obligations we have to ourselves, others, and the environment. Our spiritual destiny is to awaken to Self-knowledge, God-realization, and liberation of consciousness. Mundane and transcendental purposes can be fulfilled simultaneously. Skillful living frees energies and resources to be used constructively. It is the very best spiritual practice because it includes everything we do and everything of which we are aware. Spiritual awareness expands our consciousness and removes delusions (the results of intellectual errors), illusions (misperceptions), and all other life-suppressing conditions.

Affirm with superconscious certainty:

> My enlightened awareness energizes my mind, enlivens my
> body, and is the primary cause of my harmonious, supportive,
> personal, relationships and environmental conditions.
> I always perceive accurately, think clearly, act wisely, and
> experience orderly events and circumstances in all aspects of
> my life. I am peaceful. I am happy.

Publisher's Note:

For a more comprehensive description of ayurvedic principles and practices read *An Easy Guide to Ayurveda*; CSA Press.

> When you understand the truth of suffering, its cause, its remedy,
> and the means of its cessation ... you will walk the right path.
> Right views will be the torch that lights your way. Right aspirations
> will be your guide. Right speech will be your dwelling place on life's
> road. Your way will be straight, for it is right behavior. Your
> nourishment will be the right means of earning your livelihood.
> Right endeavors will be your steps. Right thoughts will be your breath.
> Right contemplation will provide you abiding peace.
> — *Teachings of Gautama, the Buddha*

MEDITATION PRACTICE

TECHNIQUE OF PRIMORDIAL SOUND CONTEMPLATION

> Kriya pranayama and contemplation of Om are the keys to effective meditation practice. Practice of these methods make possible the fulfillment of one's highest aspirations.
>
> *– Lahiri Mahasaya*

When a mantra (or another technique) has served the purpose of taking the meditator's attention inward and has been disregarded, meditation may then flow spontaneously and superconscious states may prevail. Or, it may be that, without an object upon which to focus attention, awareness may become passive and subject to being invaded by random thoughts, memories, and surges of emotion, causing concentration to be disturbed and fantasies to be produced by the mind.

Until concentration is focused and uninterrupted, it is important to maintain alert interest in apprehending and experiencing higher realities. For this purpose, it is most helpful to discern, hear, listen to, and contemplate the sound-current of the power of Consciousness.

> The evidential aspect of God is Om. [Sustained] meditation on Om culminates in knowledge of it and God-realization.
>
> *— yoga-sutras 1:27,28*

Sustained contemplation on Om enables the meditator to merge awareness with it, explore its aspects, and eventually transcend it to experience the reality of God.

Practice contemplative Om meditation like this:

• Use your usual technique to meditate to the stage of tranquil, thought-free awareness.
• With your awareness at the spiritual eye center and higher brain, listen inside your ears and in your head until you discern a subtle sound. When a sound is heard, endeavor to hear a subtle sound behind it. Continue until you hear a sound that does not change.
• Blend your awareness with that sound. Merge in it.
• If you perceive inner light, blend your awareness with it as you merge your awareness with the sound.
• Gently inquire into the source of sound and light.
• Continue to meditate until you perceive that you are one with Om or until, having transcended it, you experience pure awareness of Being or a perception of oneness or wholeness.

The first sounds you hear may be those which occur naturally in the inner ear. As your attention becomes more internalized, you may discern the various, subtle sound-frequencies of the vital centers (chakras) in the spinal pathway. Eventually, when you hear a constant sound, use it as a mantra. Hear and perceive it in and outside of your head. Consider it as an aspect of Om which pervades your body and the universe. Expand and merge your awareness with it. If you perceive inner light, merge your awareness in it and Om.

Some meditators perceive a golden light, or a field of dark blue with a golden halo. They may also see a brilliant white light in the blue field. The teachers of this kriya yoga tradition declare golden light to be the radiance of Om; the dark blue to be the radiance of Consciousness-Intelligence that pervades the universe; and the brilliant white light to be the radiance of Consciousness itself.

If these lights are perceived, one can be inclined to merge with the golden light of Om; the blue light of omnipresent, Cosmic Intelligence-directed Consciousness; and the white light of Consciousness from which all aspects of itself and of nature are emanated.

If inner light is not easily perceived while contemplating Om, do not despair. Light perception, while of interest, is not as important as the clarification of awareness and the emergence of Self- and God-knowledge. Light perception is more likely when the waves of thoughts and emotions are pacified and remain dormant.

Any subjective perception of mental imagery (of people or other kinds of images) should be disregarded. The purpose of meditation practice is to transcend such phenomena. They are indications that desires, restlessness, and tendencies arising from the subconscious level of the mind are still influential. Be alert and attentive when meditating, yet patient as you learn by practice to acquire control of your attention and your states of awareness.

Meditators with a dominant vata constitution may tend to be easily distracted, feel lightheaded, be overly preoccupied with subjective phenomena, or be inclined to want to receive messages from disembodied souls or to share with others the information or guidance they mistakenly think they are receiving.

Meditators with a dominant pitta constitution may tend to have dramatic subjective perceptions and mistakenly consider them to be evidence of spiritual advancement.

Meditators with a dominant kapha constitution may need to be more disciplined, to avoid becoming too passive or lethargic.

> I am dyed in the color of the Lord's name [Om],
> In a hue that can never fade;
> There is no color in the world
> That can be compared to the Lord's name.
> – *Kabir*

REVIEW OF LESSON TWO

1. What is the definition of the word *monotheism*?

    _____

2. What are the characteristics of the three modifying attributes in God, the Oversoul?

    _____

    _____

    _____

3. What is Om?

    _____

4. How are souls individualized?

    _____

5. What can you do to be Self- and God-realized?

    _____

    _____

6. Define the word *ayurveda*.

    _____

7. What is your basic mind-body constitution (the percentages of vata, pitta, and kapha characteristics?

    _____

8. Write a lifestyle routine and food plan (if necessary) that will enable your basic mind-body constitution to be maintained in a balanced state.

    _____

    _____

    _____

9. Review the guidelines for practicing the primordial sound technique. Practice it when you meditate.

PERSONAL APPLICATION

Pain and suffering which has not yet been experienced is to be avoided. Suffering is due to excessive identification with the mind and body and their processes. The objective realms, composed of elements, powers of sensation, thought, and action, and influenced by the constituent attributes of nature, serve the purpose of providing consciousness with the means for expression and liberation. – *Patanjali's yoga-sutras 2: 16 – 18*

Are you doing all that you presently know to do to help yourself experience total well-being and allow your innate knowledge and soul qualities to unfold? Are you aware of any mental attitudes, psychological conditions, or personal habits or behaviors which may be interfering with your spiritual growth? Write them here or in your personal journal. Write what you will do to overcome or renounce them.

Condition   Corrective Action

_____   _____

_____   _____

_____   _____

_____   _____

_____   _____

What else can (and will) you do to live more effectively and allow your spiritual growth to occur more rapidly?

_____

_____

_____

_____

_____

_____

Demonstrate your commitment to spiritual growth by regular superconscious meditation practice and wholesome, constructive living.

THE WISDOM OF LAHIRI MAHASAYA

One [supreme] Self is the ultimate Reality. It is the source of everything. The soul is immortal. God's attributes permeate it. Let your spiritual path be God-communion.

Restless thoughts are caused by restless movements of prana [life force].

Keeping on, keeping on; one day behold!, the divine realization.

When the waves [fluctuations] of awareness are transcended by meditation practice, consciousness is purified and oneness with the Supreme Self is realized. The phenomenal world, the truth seeker's awareness, and Supreme Consciousness, are experienced as one.

Meditation is the practice of conscious awareness of the presence of God within. It is the constant remembrance of the transcendental Spirit. God is revealed within us when our awareness is made pure by liberating it from all concepts of duality and finitude.

The mind has two states: restless and serene. When the mind is serene, the reality of God is reflected in it. God, all-pervading and eternal, transcends mind and intellect.

Meditation results in divine revelation. Then out of the reality of one's being arises the perception and realization [experience] of the pure Self, the indwelling God. Self-realization is conscious cognition of our absolute identity with God, the Self-revelation of our true nature by the illumination of our pure consciousness.

There is a subtle bond between the soul and the senses. The mind is the connecting link between the soul and the senses. Divine perceptions are acquired when the senses are spiritualized. Joy, sweetness, and exultation fill the entire being when the sense faculties are purified and inspired by the purity of the soul. The body is the holy temple. God as the indwelling soul is the deity. One who is enlightened knows this truth.

Meditation practice establishes inner balance, restores harmony to the nervous system, clarifies the mind, increases will power, and inspires constructive emotions.

Each person is responsible for his inner life—which is the creation of one's thoughts, desires, feelings and ideals.

Our lives have a twofold purpose. One is to accomplish our personal objectives; the other is to fulfill the will of God. These complement each other. Our personal desires and ideals must be in harmony with the will and purpose of God.

LESSON THREE

PHILOSOPHY

THE CATEGORIES AND PROCESSES
OF GOD'S COSMIC MANIFESTATION

Calm the waves of thoughts and emotions that distort your perception of reality. Then in superconsciousness you will behold everything as it really is. – *Paramahansa Yogananda*

For hundreds of years the subject of whether or not the beliefs and opinions of religion and science can ever be compatible has been vigorously debated. Many proponents of religious doctrine assert that their own intuition or the "revelations" described by the saints or prophets of their tradition provide them sufficient assurance to live a meaningful life. They feel that any attempt to verify what they believe might indicate doubt that would signify a lack faith. Some scientists easily blend their religious views with their acquired knowledge of the laws of nature; many say the existence of God can neither be proved nor disproved.

To bridge the gap between religion and science, what is needed is insight into the esoteric (inner) side of life that provides knowledge of Consciousness and its processes that can be proved as reliable when rationally investigated and tested, as well as personally experienced. To satisfy this need, the following explanations of the categories and processes of God's cosmic manifestation will be helpful.

It is not expected that the reader to whom these concepts are new will immediately comprehend all of them, nor is it necessary to do so. The most useful approach is to contemplate them in the light of both intuition and reason, then let understanding emerge with the passing of time. At the innermost core of our being, we already know what is true. Only when our innate knowledge is fully unfolded will it be of value because authentic.

The Godhead is emanated by an impulse from the field of pure, absolute, Supreme Consciousness. When the Godhead manifests, three primary attributes are produced within it which make possible its actions and influences: the power of attraction; the power of repulsion; and the power of transformation that results from the interactions of the first two attributes. The Godhead is self-aware, has knowledge of itself and its processes, and its intelligence-directed actions conform to its innate laws of causation.

The power of God's consciousness emanates a vibrating force (Om) which produces within itself space, time, and cosmic forces—a field of Primordial Nature which is not distinct from God because it is emanated from God.

THE PROCESSES AND CATEGORIES OF COSMIC MANIFESTATION

Field of Absolute, Pure Consciousness
Unmodified, devoid of characteristics.

God (Oversoul)
The first outward manifestation of the one Consciousness with manifesting, enlivening, and transformative characteristics.

Field of Primordial Nature
Produced by the Power of Consciousness emanated from the Godhead. Intelligence-directed vibrating force (Om) expresses as space, time, and fine cosmic forces with the potential to manifest universes. The Field of Primordial Nature (maya) produces forms and obscures (veils) the pure essence of Consciousness. Individualized aspects of Consciousness are expressed when the enlivening aspect of God interacts with the Field of Primordial Nature. Souls are individualized aspects of Consciousness with awareness blurred because of being identified with nature's characteristics and processes.

Field of Cosmic Mind
The one Mind of which all individualized minds are units, it is responsive to and conforms to mental and emotional states, thoughts, and desires. Mind and the following subtle and gross manifestations of cosmic forces are produced by the influences of the three attributes of nature. Souls produce and attract sheaths (bodies) through which to function in causal, astral, and physical realms in accord with their inclinations, desires, or needs.

Subtle Essences of the Five Senses
Smell, taste, sight, touch, hearing which make possible the soul's perception of external phenomena and circumstances.

Subtle Essences of the Five Modes of Action
Assimilation, elimination, reproduction, mobility, dexterity.

Subtle Essences of the Five Elements
Ether (space with cosmic forces), air (circulating influence), fire (transformative influence), water (moistening), earth (solidifying).

Gross Manifestation of the Essences of the Five Elements
Expressive in and as the mundane realm.

In the beginning was the Word [Logos, Om], and the Word was with God, and the Word was God. All things were made by God, and without God was not any thing made that was made.
New Testament / Gospel of St. John 1:1 & 3

Along with Om, a surge of repulsion causes a magnetized field of Cosmic Individuality to be simultaneously manifested. Its positive pole, Cosmic Intelligence, attracts it to the field of pure Existence; its negative pole, Cosmic Mind, repels it. The four aspects of Cosmic Individuality—awareness which "feels" (perceives) sensations; the illusional sense of independent existence; Cosmic Intelligence; and Cosmic Mind—are the same characteristics which define the non-cosmic units of individualized Consciousness which, when further involved with nature's processes, are referred to as souls.

Five electric currents are produced in the field of Cosmic Individuality: one from the middle, two from the two extremities, and two from the gaps or spaces between the middle of the two extremities. These five currents, the causative essences of all that is manifested, comprise the Cosmic Causal Body of God. Produced in the field of Individualized Consciousness, they are endowed with its three attributes.

The positive (polarity) aspects of the five electric currents are the essences of the organs of perception: smell, taste, sight, touch, and hearing. They are attributes of the mind.

The neutralizing aspects of the five electric currents are the essences of the organs of action which make possible excretion of waste products, generation, mobility, dexterity, and speech. They are attributes of the life force body of living things.

The negative (polarity) aspects of the five electric currents are the essences that make possible the manifestation of the objects of sense perception which are smelled, tasted, seen, touched, and heard.

The above-described fifteen aspects, plus intelligence, and mind, comprise the fine material body of souls.

When the five essences that make physical manifestation possible combine in various ways, five forms of gross matter are produced: space with cosmic forces; gaseous matter; fiery or transformative characteristics; liquids; and solids. The three constituent attributes of nature produce the elements. Sattva produces space; sattva and rajas produce gaseous substance; rajas produces fire; rajas and tamas produce water; tamas produces earth. Each form of gross matter has a minute part of the other four subtle element essences. Processes that occur in living forms of gross matter are governed by three element-influences (doshas). Vata dosha, with space and air characteristics, causes movement and circulation. Pitta dosha, with fire and water characteristics, causes transformative effects. Kapha dosha, with water and earth characteristics, provides cohesiveness and stability.

The five gross substances, the fifteen subtle essences, mind, intelligence, the sense of individuality, and the core consciousness (sometimes referred to as the heart) are the twenty-four principles that make possible the categories and processes of God's cosmic manifestation.

Primordial Nature is referred to as *maya*: that which measures, defines, and produces forms. Maya, though illusory when misunderstood, is not unreal; it is produced by interactions of cosmic forces emanated from the Godhead. Because it produces forms, it is sometimes referred to as the Divine Mother or Mother Nature. Because it partially obscures or veils the "light" of Consciousness, in some philosophical systems it is referred to as "the darkness." An understanding of the categories and processes of God's cosmic manifestation provides knowledge that one Reality, interacting only with itself, exists.

THE EIGHT ASPECTS OF GOD, THE SEVEN
FIELDS OF COSMIC MANIFESTATION, AND
THE FIVE COVERINGS OF CONSCIOUSNESS

Of the eight aspects of God, seven are subjective; one is objective. Six subjective aspects, pervasive and specialized, are instrumental in regulating the processes of manifestation, preservation and transformation at causal, astral, and physical levels. The seventh subjective aspect is the omnipresent presence of God which is accessible to devotees who aspire to have a relationship with God.

Cosmic Individuality, the eighth and only objective aspect, is instrumental in causing the universe to manifest and persist just as a soul's individualized consciousness in relationship to its mind, body, and personal circumstances is instrumental in causing them to manifest and persist.

The seven fields (realms) of cosmic manifestation are:

- The field of God, the Oversoul aspect.
- The field of the radiant, enlivening aspect of God.
- Primordial Nature: Om, space, time, and cosmic forces.
- Cosmic Individuality, where the radiant, enlivening aspect of God blends with the field of Primordial Nature to individualize units of itself (referred to as souls).
- The causal field composed of magnetism, electric currents, and fine essences with potential to manifest subtle and gross phenomena.
- The astral field of life forces.
- The field of gross matter, the physical universe.

The universe is an electromagnetic field containing a specific amount of energy. The quantity of energy of a universe is constant. Although it can be transformed, it can never be increased nor decreased. One force, the power of Consciousness, manifests as all of the forces that can be observed and categorized in the field of nature. The electromagnetic spectrum is the total range of radiation with wavelengths that include cosmic rays, photons, gamma rays, x-rays, ultraviolet radiation, visible light, infrared radiation, microwaves, radio waves, heat, and electric currents. At the gross level, matter is composed of atoms with subatomic particles. Protons have a positive charge, are stable, and have more mass than electrons which are unstable and have a negative charge. The energy of matter is held together by a nuclear force which, when sufficiently disturbed, allows an explosive electrical force to be released.

When the essences of the organs of perception, action, and objects of perception are emanated, five sheaths (coverings) of Consciousness are produced:

• The bliss sheath, so-named because it is the basis of feeling, sensation, and enjoyment.
• The intelligence sheath, which produces the faculty of intellectual determination.
• The mind sheath, with the subtle essences of the organs of perception. The first three sheaths comprise the soul's causal body.
• The life force (prana) sheath, the astral body with the subtle essences of subtle organs of action.
• The gross material sheath, with subtle essences of the objects of perception which make possible the emergence of physical forms nourished by food and other forces of nature.

When all of the subtle essences that make possible the manifestation of a universe and various forms of life have been fully expressed, the attracting influence of the Godhead causes them to interact. A physical universe is then manifested.

When the action of the attracting influence of the Godhead causes the cosmic sheath of life force with its organs of action to be unveiled, vegetation emerges on planets with ideal conditions to nourish it.

When the cosmic sheath with subtle essences of organs of action is unveiled, the animal kingdom emerges.

When the cosmic sheaths of intelligence and mind are unveiled, human beings emerge.

When a devotee's aspiration to be enlightened supported by right spiritual practice unveils the innermost sheath which obscures awareness of being, he or she becomes Self-realized.

When the illusional sense of independent existence is removed, the soul becomes God-realized. All of the delusions and illusions which formerly prevailed are absent.

THE UNIVERSE FUNCTIONS IN ACCORD WITH ORDERLY LAWS OF CAUSE AND EFFECT

Supportive influences arising within the Godhead empower evolutionary trends that determine the fate of a universe. Our universe is still in the infant stage. In Vedic scriptures, its life span is estimated to be a little more than three trillion solar years in duration, of which fifteen billion years (approximately) have passed since its origin.

In 1894, in his book *The Holy Science*, Sri Yukteswar explained how a 24,000-year equinoctial cycle influenced by cosmic forces radiating from the center of our galaxy relates to the present Era. Each of two 12,000-year cycles (one ascending, one descending) within the 24,000-year cycle have four Ages (*yugas*). The first ascending Era within the longer 12,000-year cycle is described as 1200 years of confusion (*kali*). It is followed by 2400 years during which the majority of the planet's human inhabitants are aware of and can apply the electrical and magnetic properties of nature. Next, is a 3600-year Era during which human mental capacities are highly developed. The last ascending Era of 4800 years is an Age of global spiritual enlightenment. After 4800 years have passed, a descending cycle begins, with the characteristics of these Ages manifesting in reverse order as the awareness of most human beings becomes gradually blurred and their intellectual and intuitive powers are diminished.

According to this theory, as of the year 2000, 200 years of an ascending 2400-year cycle of discovery and practical application of electrical and magnetic properties have transpired. The Mental Age will begin in 4100 of the Current Era, to be followed by an Age of spiritual enlightenment which will begin in the year 7700. (For a detailed explanation, see *yuga* in the Glossary).

Teachers of this kriya yoga tradition emphasize that, regardless of external conditions which influence the general population, a person who chooses to do so can awaken to spiritual enlightenment and be impervious to them. Now that more people on the planet are able to comprehend the existence of subtle forces which influence mental and physiological processes, kriya yoga meditation methods can be more widely taught and effectively used. Right use of these procedures rapidly refines the physical body, purifies the intellect, and illumines the mind of the dedicated practitioner.

Since before the beginning of recorded history, doomsday prophets have been uttering dire pronouncements of impending disaster for our planet and its inhabitants, and they have invariably been wrong. As we begin another millennium, their voices are still heard, and will continue to be heard until fantasy and ignorance are replaced by rational thinking and accurate knowledge of evolutionary processes.

Insecure or dysfunctional people are confused, afraid, and habitually pessimistic. Healthy-minded people are courageous, curious, optimistic, and appreciative of the opportunities for learning and experience that the beneficial changes which are occurring will provide for them and the majority of the human family.

In 1830, the global human population was one billion (one thousand million). A hundred years later (1930) it was two billion. Forty-five years later (1975) it had doubled to four billion. Twenty-five years later (year 2000) it was six billion. At the present growth rate of approximately two hundred thousand new people a day (the rate of births exceeds that of deaths) or eighty million annually, by 2010 another billion will be added. Unless human population growth is soon stabilized, by 2050 it is estimated that 10 billion people will have to compete for food, water, and other natural resources.

Most of the population growth will be in undeveloped regions of the world where the quality of life for human inhabitants is already substandard. It is estimated that more than one billion people are presently existing on the equivalent of one dollar a day and at least that many do not have access to pure drinking water. The population increase, pollution of the earth's atmosphere by the growing use of fossil fuels, soil depletion, diminished water reserves, imprudent cutting of forests, and the possibility of global warming represent major challenges to the welfare of the planet and all forms of life. These matters need to be confronted with meaningful solutions.

Of utmost importance is the spiritual education of receptive people of all ages throughout the world. When people lack knowledge of their true nature and their relationship to the whole, they tend to mistakenly presume themselves to be mortal, material beings and are inclined to be self-centered, addicted to illusional opinions and destructive behaviors, and inconsiderate of the welfare of themselves, others, and nature. If religious, but without higher understanding, they may think that personal, environmental, and social problems can only be solved by divine intervention, and may be inclined to wait for a unique person with exceptional wisdom and powers to arrive on the scene or a timely event to occur that might adjust matters in their favor instead of playing a positive role that would be helpful.

I well remember a comment made by Paramahansa Yogananda in regard to the current trend of planetary evolution, to which he referred as "God's will" (innate inclination). Speaking informally to a few disciples, he said, "God's will, will be done, regardless of whether we cooperate with it or not. But how much better it is to cooperate, for when we do, we are better able to serve others and our own spiritual evolution is quickened."

If a light of a thousand suns should suddenly appear in the sky, such brilliance might faintly resemble the splendor of that great Being.
– *Bhagavad Gita 11:12*

LIFESTYLE GUIDELINES

FULFILL YOUR LIFE-ENHANCING DESIRES

Self-discipline, will power, noble desire, controlled speech, devotion, steadfastness, courage, patience, cheerfulness, and simplicity and moderation in natural living are some of the basic prerequisites of a spiritual and happy life. The senses should be used to fulfill their normal functions, always with spiritual idealism while abiding in God-communion. Perceptions of the phenomenal world become spiritual experiences when the senses are inspired and governed by the soul.

– *Lahiri Mahasaya*

desire Latin *desiderare*; to wish or want.
desirable Worth wanting or doing; pleasing; valuable; advantageous.

Just as we cannot live effectively without performing actions which are essential for our well-being, we cannot live effectively without having desires. Constructive, wholesome desires are compatible with spiritual aspiration because their fulfillment enables needs to be satisfied and meaningful purposes to be accomplished.

For the person who wants to live effectively and be Self- and God-realized, the desires to be renounced are:

• Unrealistic desires which cannot be fulfilled.
• Obsessive desires which nurture fantasies and cause psychological distress.
• Desires which, if fulfilled, would contribute to personal misfortune, harm others or the environment, or serve no purpose of value.
• Desires which arise because of restlessness, confusion, boredom, or an inclination to imitate the behaviors of others whose life-purposes are different from one's own.

The fulfillment of desires which improve the quality of our lives, nurture our spiritual growth, and benefit others and the environment is acceptable and will not cause misfortune. The most efficient way to remove nonuseful or harmful desires is to neutralize and replace them with constructive desires. This can be accomplished by mastery of attention, thoughts, and emotions, and by intentional performance of actions which are of value. Until proficiency in Self- (soul) directed behavior is acquired, it can be helpful to emulate the mental states and behaviors of role models whose lives are exemplary.

There should be no reluctance in regard to having life-enhancing desires fulfilled. If life is not lived effectively and enjoyably, frustration, emotional distress, psychological conflicts, physical problems, and functional disabilities may be experienced.

HOW TO HAVE LIFE-ENHANCING DESIRES FULFILLED WITH MINIMUM EFFORT

• Accurately define your needs and meaningful goals and purposes. Be specific. Write them in a private notebook. Write what you can and will do to accomplish them.

• Discern the difference between necessary, life-enhancing desires and desires which are not necessary or important. Focus your attention and actions on having necessary, life-enhancing desires fulfilled. Disregard all other desires.

• At all times, be aware of the fact that you abide in the wholeness of God and that your mind is a part of a Universal Mind which is responsive to your desires and needs.

Until you are always aware that God's wholeness includes you and that your mind is one with Universal Mind, frequently quiet your thoughts and emotions. Rest in the silence until you are soul- and God-centered, peaceful, and confident. It does not require extreme effort to do this. Remind yourself that because you are an individualized aspect of one field of omnipresent Consciousness, you abide in it.

When desires arise in your awareness, discriminate between those which are in accord with your ultimate aims in life and those which are not. Allow life-enhancing desires to be impelling; discard all other desires. Sometimes a nonuseful desire may persist because of the force of subconscious tendencies or habit. Replace such desires with constructive aspirations and concentrate your thoughts and actions to accomplish useful purposes. Troublesome desires and inclinations will be weakened and dissolved. The energy formerly confined by them will be released and used for higher purposes. By overcoming destructive and nonuseful subconscious tendencies, you will become strong and self-confident.

To have your needs satisfied and your wholesome desires fulfilled, you have only to learn to cooperate with the universal, impersonal laws of mind and Consciousness which determine that every cause produces a corresponding effect. The thoughts you habitually think, the states of consciousness you maintain, and the effective actions you skillfully perform (when necessary) will then actualize (manifest) the results you desire.

Actions which are not impelled by a clearly defined purpose are not as productive as actions motivated by clarity of purpose reinforced by awareness of your relationship to God and the universe.

If physical actions are required to assist the fulfillment of desires, when you know what to do, do it. If actions are required and you do not know how to proceed, learn what to do. It may be that only subjective actions—an adjustment of viewpoint and of mental and emotional states—will be required. Remember that you are a spiritual being, superior to your thoughts, moods, and circumstances.

Be responsible for your behaviors: for what you think, how you feel, and what you do. Don't complain, make excuses for irresponsible behavior, or think or say that life isn't fair or that God doesn't care about you. Immature mental attitudes, unregulated emotions, and reluctance to exercise will power (the ability to make decisions and implement plans to accomplish goals and purposes) are debilitating behaviors. Think rationally. Stabilize your emotions. Learn to make wise decisions. If you make a mistake, you will know what not to do in the future. Cheerfully and skillfully implement plans that will enable you to accomplish your purposes without being mentally or emotionally attached to your actions or to their results. It is natural for you to be healthy, happy, prosperous, and successful.

Avoid thinking that when your needs are satisfied and your desires are fulfilled you will have more time to devote to spiritual study and practice. Educate yourself about spiritual matters and nurture your soul qualities while you are learning to live effectively. The more spiritually aware you are, the more inwardly fulfilled you will be and the easier it will be to live effectively. You will soon discover that your Self-awareness, increasingly accurate perception of the reality of God, and improved knowledge of the laws of cause and effect enable you to live without limitations of any kind.

Desires are inclined to be self-fulfilling. When you discern an impulse of desire, know that it is making an impression in Universal Mind which is responsive to it. If this natural process of impulse and response is not interrupted by an opposing urge or desire or by your inappropriate actions, the causative influence of desire will produce an effect which corresponds to it. Whatever is needed for the outcome to occur will be provided by the universe through the medium of Universal Mind.

Your circumstances are always conformed to your perception of them. To change them, perceive and acknowledge possibilities. Use these procedures to assist the process of fulfillment of desire:

• When you discern an impulse of desire and want it to be fulfilled, *gently intend* that it be fulfilled. Visualize the outcome but do not use will power to force the issue. There is no need to be demanding or aggressive. Too much effort indicates doubt in regard to the ability of the universe to satisfy needs or desires. *Gently intend* for ideal results to occur, with an awareness of certainty. Trust the process. Have faith in the laws of cause and effect. Be happy and thankful.

• Meditate until the mind is still and you are peaceful. Listen to the inner sound of Om and merge your awareness with it. Float your desire in the Om vibration. Paramahansa Yogananda taught: "Desires are [spontaneously] realized when you are in conscious contact with the Cosmic vibration [of Om]."

Coordinate your desires with your aspirations be healthy, happy, secure, creatively functional, prosperous, and Self- and God-realized. Avoid thinking that your experiences are primarily determined by karma or by planetary, cultural, social, or environmental influences. Karmic influences (*samskaras*: impressions, the results of previous thoughts, desires, and reactions) can be modified, changed, and transcended by:

• Positive thinking and intentional, goal-oriented actions.
• Acquiring experiences which are life-enhancing.
• Meditation practice which allows superconscious influences to beneficially influence the mind and body.

Repeated superconscious episodes remove the meditator's awareness from mental states, weaken destructive drives and tendencies, and leave constructive impressions in the mind. When only constructive karmic tendencies are dominant, the devotee is inclined to think and act wisely and to experience only supportive circumstances. Eventually, even the influences of constructive karma are transcended.

• Associating with spiritually aware people and being nurtured by harmonious, wholesome environmental conditions.
• The impulses of grace which arise from within the core of one's being as the result of aspiration, devotion, cultivation of awareness of the presence of God, and regular superconscious meditation.

External influences need not be unduly influential. Be insightful and illusion-free. View your progressive awakening to higher levels of understanding and the unfoldment of your functional abilities as a great adventure in learning and growing. Anchored in Self-knowledge and God-awareness, live in harmony with the forces of nature.

Seek first the kingdom of God, and live righteously;
and all these things shall be added to you.
– *New Testament / Matthew 6:33 / modern translation*

MEDITATION PRACTICE

TECHNIQUE FOR CONSCIOUS EXPANSION OF AWARENESS

> Devotees who [clearly] comprehend the eternal nature of the supreme Self renounce all attachments. Meditating with one-pointed concentration, they dissolve their awareness in God.
> — *Sri Yukteswar*

Use this technique to detach your attention from the senses, expand your awareness beyond the boundaries of your body and mind, and consciously realize (apprehend and experience) the reality of your true nature and of God.

Meditate in your usual way until your mind is calm. Rest there for a while, then practice this technique:

• Look into the spiritual eye. Visualize a ball of dark blue light. Identify your awareness with it. Feel yourself to be it.

• As conscious, blue light, expand until you fill your head. Expand until you fill your body. Expand until you extend beyond the boundaries of your body and your body is within you.

• As conscious, blue light, expand until you fill the room and everything in the room is within you.

• Continue to expand until your community with its buildings, trees, people, creatures—everything—floats in your awareness.

• Expand until Planet Earth is floating in your awareness. Mentally "see" it turning on its axis and moving in its orbit.

• Expand until the sun and planets of our solar system float within your awareness. Expand until the galaxy—100,000 light years from one edge to the other, with its billions of suns—is within you.

• Expand until the physical universe with its billions of galaxies is floating within your field of awareness.

• Listen to the sound of the Om vibration. Contemplate the field of Primordial Nature: Om, space, time, and cosmic forces. Merge your awareness in Om.

• Contemplate the source of Om: the Godhead or Oversoul. Examine it, merge your awareness with it.

• Contemplate absolute, pure Consciousness (existence-being). Let any remaining perception of an illusional sense of existing apart from the reality of pure Consciousness dissolve. Remain in that clear, aware experience for as long as it persists.

Imagination is only used for the purpose of expanding awareness to the stage of meditating in the Om vibration. Merge with Om, the manifesting power of Consciousness, then contemplate its source (God) while aspiring to experience pure awareness of being.

Paramahansa Yogananda often recommended the practice of this technique. It is enjoyable to experience and provides opportunities for meaningful discovery which are ordinarily not available when one's awareness is confined to habitual ways of thinking and perceiving.

Be curious when exploring inner realms. Be discerningwhile using your powers of imagination and intuition. Avoid fantasy.

RECOMMENDED ROUTINES

1. First, acquire skill in practicing the technique, moving through the stages in successive order until you are contemplating the heart (core) of Consciousness. This can be done in five minutes or less. Rest there for as long as desired, then conclude the practice session.

2. When you can practice the technique easily, move through the stages more slowly. Vividly experience each level as fully as possible. Remain absorbed in conscious awareness of existence-being for a longer duration of time.

3. From time to time, after resting at the stage of existence-being, as you return to body and mind awareness, explore and examine the categories and processes of God's cosmic manifestation: from God to Om; the Fields of Primordial Nature and Cosmic Individuality; the emanation of subtle essences of perception, action, and the objects of perception; and the manifestation of gross matter.

Note: when doing this, while at the stage of Om-perception, if you have needs to be satisfied or desires to be fulfilled, float them in Om with a feeling of certainty.

During longer meditation sessions, use any of these techniques when you need to refocus your attention or when you are inclined to practice them. They can enable you to become more cosmic conscious.

With this technique, as with all meditation procedures, relax into your practice. While being alert and intentional, avoid assertiveness and impatience. Attune yourself to the supportive impulses of grace which will assist your meditation practice, purify your mind, and clarify your awareness.

Affirm With Conviction
Established in knowledge of what is true,
I live freely in harmony with the rhythms of life.

REVIEW OF LESSON THREE

1. How is the Godhead (Oversoul) emanated?

    _____

2. What are the four aspects of Cosmic Individuality?

    1 _____   2 _____

    3 _____   4 _____

3. Of what is the Cosmic Causal Body of God composed?

    _____

4. Carefully examine the chart of cosmic manifestation on page 50.

5. List the seven fields (realms) of cosmic manifestation.

    1 _____   2 _____

    3 _____   4 _____

    5 _____   6 _____

    7 _____

6. List the five sheaths (coverings) of individualized Consciousness (soul).

    1 _____   2 _____

    3 _____   4 _____

    5 _____

7. Review the meditation technique for conscious expansion of your awareness. Include it in your meditation practice session at least once a week.

PERSONAL APPLICATION

1. Write a clearly defined list of life-enhancing desires you would like to have fulfilled.

    _____

    _____

    _____

    _____

    _____

    _____

2. Sit quietly in a meditative state for a few minutes. In your mind's eye, see yourself with your desires fulfilled. At the innermost level of your being, *feel* the reality of fulfillment. If you do not know what to desire, envision yourself as now having everything you need for your highest good. Feel whole, complete, satisfied, and happy.

3. If you know what to do to actualize your desires, do it. If you do not know what to do, continue to *believe* and *feel* that your desires are already fulfilled. What is established in your mind and awareness is blended with Cosmic Mind and must manifest. After meditation practice, listen to Om; merge your awareness with it and float your desires in it. Everything in the universe emerges from Om (the primordial power of Consciousness). Everything you need is contained in it.

4. If time is a factor because of having to implement causative actions or to acquire skills or knowledge, hold fast to your vision of possibilities. Be optimistic. Be patient.

5. Be receptive and responsive to the unplanned good fortune that life can and will provide for you. Often, the universe knows what is best for you even when you do not.

Affirm with soul-aware conviction:
Established in conscious awareness of the wholeness of life
I am spiritually aware, mentally alert, emotionally peaceful,
physically healthy, and abundantly prosperous. I enjoy
supportive personal relationships and am always attuned
to the creative processes of the universe.

THE WISDOM OF THE BHAGAVAD GITA

This same ancient yoga [way of knowledge and practice] is now declared by me to you, for you are my disciple and friend. This is indeed the supreme secret. – 4:3

Interpretation: *This same knowledge of the one Consciousness and its processes, inaccessible to the undiscerning, is immediately Self-revealed when the devotee is prepared to apprehend it.*

Although I am unborn and imperishable, and the ruler of all living things, established in my own nature I manifest by my own creative power. – 4:6

Interpretation: *Supreme Consciousness is self-existent and eternal, the governing principle of cosmic and life processes. Established in its transcendent state, it freely expresses by its own limitless power.*

Whenever righteousness decreases and unrighteousness increases, I manifest myself. For the protection of the virtuous, for the removal of nonvirtue, and to restore righteousness, I come into manifestation from Age to Age. – 4:7,8

Interpretation: *When righteousness [elevating influences] decreases and unrighteousness [confusion and inertia] increases, supreme Consciousness emanates illuminating influences to enliven and nurture the processes of evolution.*

That one who knows the truth of my divine manifestations and actions, when departing from the body is not born again; that soul comes to me. – 4:9

Interpretation: *One who comprehends the reality of supreme Consciousness and its actions and influences, awakens from delusions and illusions of births and deaths because of being established in realization of wholeness.*

Aspiring unto me only, resorting only to me, many from whom greed, fear, and anger have departed, purified by the discipline of knowledge, have realized me. – 4:10

Interpretation: *With attention absorbed in pure consciousness, abiding in it at all times, many souls, with all obstacles to spiritual awakening having been overcome or removed, and established in truth-knowledge, have awakened to absolute realization of God.*

In whatever ways truth seekers take refuge in me, I provide them grace. Devotees of God everywhere follow my path. – 4:11

Interpretation: *However spiritual aspirants turn to God, redemptive grace nurtures them. Regardless of their outer form of endeavor or practice [in accord with their personal capacity to learn or to unfold their innate potential], firmly resolved souls with knowledge and devotion adhere to the eternal way of righteousness.*

Actions do not bind the devotee who has renounced them by the practice of yoga, whose doubts have been banished by knowledge, and who is established in Self-knowledge. – 4:41

LESSON FOUR

PHILOSOPHY

UNDERSTANDING YOUR TRUE NATURE

God is the ocean of Spirit; we are like waves that rise and fall on the ocean's surface. To one involved in the drama of relative life who is attached to success and fearful of failure, attached to good health and fearful of illness, attached to physical existence and fearful of death, human experiences appear to be the only reality. To one who is established in nonattachment, everything is perceived as God. – *Paramahansa Yogananda*

Because souls are individualized aspects of one Consciousness in relationship to cosmic forces which comprise the field of nature and its varied expressions, all unenlightened souls are innately impelled to have their awareness restored to wholeness. Although they may try to experience fulfillment by satisfying only their emotional needs, sense urges, or personality-based desires, until they ardently aspire to be Self- and God-realized and conform their lives to that ideal, they cannot be truly happy.

When souls identify with a mind after they are individualized, some retain a clear state of awareness; many become partially deluded and confused; others become so unconscious that they believe themselves to be material creatures. The four characteristics of a soul identified with Primordial Nature and its manifestations are 1) blurred awareness; 2) the illusional idea that it exists separate from God; 3) diminished mental capacity; 4) flawed powers of intelligence.

Souls are not sent by God into involvement with mundane realms to learn or to acquire experience. They are inclined to be attracted to relationships and circumstances which correspond to their states of awareness (whether blurred or clear), mental states, desires or urges, and capacity to perceive and function. Once this fact is known, more desirable relationships and circumstances can be chosen and experienced by nurturing spiritual awareness and improving mental and functional abilities.

Souls which are very confused may remain involved with gross astral and physical realms for thousands of years. They are attracted to a physical body, live in a semiconscious dream state, and make a transition to an astral realm when the physical body dies. After a brief astral sojourn, impelled by the force of their desires or attracted to the physical realm because of habit, they reincarnate.

Paramahansa Yogananda once said, "It wouldn't help [most] people to remember their past incarnations. Observe how many are bound by their habits. Almost everything they do is predictable. As they grow older, they [tend to] become more settled in their modes of thinking, feeling, and behaving. They [may] need an opportunity to forget what they have done, to start anew. [For them] with a new beginning, there is hope for improvement."

A person intent on the spiritual path does not need to know the specific circumstances of his or her previous incarnations. It is of more value to use this incarnation to awaken to Self- and God-knowledge.

THE SOUL'S RELATIONSHIP TO THE PHYSICAL BODY AND THE SEVEN MAJOR VITAL CENTERS IN THE BRAIN AND SPINE

Soul force (prana) flows into the body through the medulla oblongata at the base of the brain. From there it goes to the brain and downward through a series of vital astral centers referred to as *chakras* (wheels) through which life forces are distributed throughout the body to enliven it and perform various functions. When prana flows freely, health prevails. When its flows are weak or imbalanced, physical or psychological discomfort or dysfunction may occur. The five aspects of prana in the body are described as:

1. Upward flowing (*udana*). Seated in the throat, it contributes to speech and all upward flowing actions that occur in the body, and to the upward flowing of awareness, especially when meditating.

2. Breath of life (*prana*). Seated in the chest, it regulates respiration: inhalation and exhalation. The word used for this aspect is the same as used when referring to the primary life force.

3. Pervasive (*samana*). Seated in the stomach and intestines, it regulates digestion, assimilation, and biochemical processes.

4. Downward flowing (*apana*). Seated below the navel, it regulates elimination of the body's waste products and supports respiration.

5. Diffused (*vyana*). It pervades the body and regulates the actions of other aspects of prana.

Soul force in the body which is not yet fully expressive is referred to as *kundalini* (coiled, dormant potential). When it awakens because of the soul's desire to actualize its potential, the cultivation of devotion, meditation practice, or the actions of grace, it contributes to psychological transformation, physical regeneration, and clarification of awareness. Unfortunately, in recent years, erroneous information about this "power of Consciousness" has been widely published. Symptoms of neurosis and psychosis dramatized by some individuals who are psychologically disturbed are inaccurately diagnosed as being signs of premature kundalini awakening. When this soul force becomes influential, its effects are entirely constructive: more energy, improved health, psychological stability, improved mental and intellectual skills, exceptional powers of perception, and enhanced functional abilities.

In yogic literature, the seven major chakras are symbolically described as lotus blossoms with their petals opened and turned upward when the currents of prana flow toward the brain.

1. The first chakra (*muladhara, foundation*) at the base of the spine represents the earth element essence. Its taste (which may be experienced in the mouth or throat when meditating or when its frequencies influence biochemical processes) is sweet; its color is yellow; its sound-frequency is like the noise made by restless bees. Psychological states related to it usually indicate the influences of restlessness, insecurity, confusion, and attachments. Behaviors may reflect fearfulness, uncertainty, delusion, greed, or anger when needs are not met or desires are thwarted. Young children who are learning to adapt to new circumstances which are not yet understood may also express these characteristics. Because awareness is blurred and fragmented, the religious concepts or convictions of a person whose awareness is identified with this chakra are usually traditional. The primary concerns are physical survival and security.

2. The second chakra (*svadhisthan, abode of the self*) at the sacral region of the spine represents the water element essence. Its taste is astringent; its color is white; its sound-frequency is flutelike. Psychological states related to it usually indicate the influences of desire, sensuousness, superficial curiosity, and inclinations to discover one's self-identity. Behaviors may be expressed as overt attempts to reach out, to "touch" or communicate with others and the environment, increased sensitivity, fantasy, or role-playing. Adolescents learning to relate to and experience the world may also express these characteristics. Religious or philosophical views of a person whose awareness is identified with this chakra are seldom clearly defined. Because the faculty of discriminative intelligence is not yet sufficiently developed to enable one to discern the difference between what is real and of value and what is not, a "truth seeker" may be dysfunctional or neurotic, have addictive personality traits, or be inclined to be preoccupied with phenomena, illusional perceptions, irrational belief systems, and nonuseful spiritual practices.

3. The third chakra (*manipura, the city of gems*) at the lumbar region of the spine represents the fire element essence. Its taste is bitter; its color is red; its sound-frequency is similar to the sound of a harp. The psychological state related to it indicates egocentric drives and inclinations and strong powers of self-centered will. Because of a pronounced sense of independent selfhood (egoism), behaviors may be expressed as attempts to demonstrate personal power, to compete with others, or acquire recognition or status. Young adults inclined to dramatize their independence and come to terms with the world may express these characteristics. A person whose awareness is identified with this chakra

and who is interested in metaphysical studies and spiritual practices may be inclined to be self-serving, to want the material and psychological benefits that might result from the acquisition of higher knowledge and clarified awareness without having to purify the ego.

4. The fourth chakra (*anahata*, unstruck sound) at the dorsal region of the spine represents the air element essence. Its taste is sour; its color is blue; its sound-frequency is like the flowing peal of a gong. The psychological state related to it is aspiration to spiritual growth, which may be frustrated by flawed powers of discernment. Behaviors may be expressed as lifestyle changes, a change in direction in life, restlessness and uncertainty because of a feeling that something important to one's life is missing, the development of conscience and a sincere desire to be Self-realized. Middle-aged adults who want to live a more meaningful life often express these characteristics. When awareness is identified with this chakra, if aspiration to spiritual growth is sincere, a person may be ready for discipleship training. At this stage, superconscious states can more easily be experienced.

5. The fifth chakra (*vishudda*, the pure) at the cervical region of the spine opposite the throat represents the ether element essence. Its taste is pungent; its color is grey or misty with sparkling points of light; its sound-frequency is as thunder or the ocean's roar. The psychological state related to it is ardent aspiration to directly apprehend higher knowledge. It is a common characteristic of adults who are withdrawing from mundane duties and relationships and are aware of the fact that their earth-life is soon to be concluded. When a spiritual aspirant's awareness is identified with this chakra, innate knowledge and cosmic conscious states can more easily unfold.

6. The sixth chakra (*ajna*, command, that which rules or regulates), the spiritual eye between the eyebrows, is the reflected light of vital forces in the medulla oblongata at the base of the brain. It may be perceived as a ball of brilliant, white light, or as a dark, blue field of light with a golden halo. A glistening, starlike, white light may be perceived in the blue field. Behaviors indicate that one is peaceful, insightful, soul-content, and willing to share knowledge with others who aspire to spiritual growth. Spiritual aspirants with awareness identified with this chakra can awaken to Self-realization.

7. The seventh chakra (*sahasrara*, "thousand rayed") at (though not confined to) the higher brain. It has the radiance as of a brilliant white light. When awareness is identified with the sixth and seventh chakras, superconsciousness prevails. When a meditator's attention is focused at these chakras, the sound of Om may be heard prior to experiencing transcendent states of awareness. Behaviors are always compassionate and selfless. Liberation of consciousness occurs.

PRACTICE THIS SIMPLE ROUTINE

Harmonious actions of the life forces contribute to physical health, psychological well-being, and mental peace. To encourage the life forces to flow freely and perform their functions, specific pranayama (*pran*, life force; *ayama*, unrestrained) practices may be used.

One of the basic routines is practiced in this manner:

· Sit upright. Inhale deeply. Exhale. Relax.
· With a finger, close the right nostril. Inhale smoothly through the left nostril. Pause for a moment.
· Close the left nostril and exhale smoothly through the right nostril. Pause for a moment.
· Inhale through the right nostril. Pause for a moment. Exhale through the left nostril.

Novice practitioners can do this simple pranayama eight to ten times. Because the left nostril is related to the prana channel along the left side of the spine, and the right nostril is related to prana channel along the right side of the spine, this practice directly effects the flows of life forces that move through them.

The current of life force flowing in the left channel has a cooling effect; the current flowing in the right channel has a warming effect. They are referred to, respectively, as lunar (moon) and solar (sun) currents. They alternate in intensity for a duration of approximately two hours when a person is physically and psychologically healthy and can be disrupted or imbalanced by physical illness, psychological distress, trauma, and irregular lifestyle patterns. When the left current is dominant, the right hemisphere of the brain is more active. When the right current is dominant, the left hemisphere of the brain is more active. When the flows of prana in the spinal pathway are balanced, the processes related to both sides of the brain tend to be coordinated. Mental and emotional calmness prevails and it is easier for a person to be both rational and intuitive. This pranayama can be used prior to meditation practice to elicit physical relaxation and improve concentration.

The soul, when it has driven away from itself all that is
contrary to the divine will [impulse], becomes transformed in God.
— St. John of the Cross

LIFESTYLE GUIDELINES

BE PROSPEROUS IN ALL ASPECTS OF YOUR LIFE

Very few people know that the wholeness of God extends fully to this physical realm. – *Mahavatar Babaji*

prosper Word source, Latin *prosperare*. To make fortunate; to be successful; to have favorable circumstances.

Every devotee of God should be prosperous. The spiritual basis of prosperity is flawless awareness of wholeness.

We are truly prosperous when we:

• Are always spiritually aware.
• Are mentally, emotionally, and physically healthy.
• Have harmonious, mutually satisfying relationships with people with whom we live or associate.
• Can confidently, skillfully, and appropriately relate to the world and its ongoing events and circumstances.
• Can efficiently and enjoyably perform our duties and consistently accomplish purposes which are of real value.
• Always have our life-enhancing desires easily fulfilled.
• Always have resources which enable us to live effectively.

Every devotee of God should be prosperous. If you are not yet in a continuous flow of fortunate events and circumstances, open your mind and awareness to the highest good that life can and will provide for you. Do not think that there is value in being poor, ill, mentally troubled, emotionally distressed, limited or restricted, or dysfunctional. Do not cling to the irrational opinion that only by thinking positive thoughts, praying sincerely, or meditating that all of your problems will be solved.

While nurturing your spiritual growth to clarify and expand your awareness, also perform decisive, constructive actions. Renounce all thoughts and feelings of limitation. Be a possibility-thinker: imagine what is best for you and reinforce that mental picture with faith.

• If you need physical healing, find out what you need to do to be healed and do it.
• If you need peace of mind and emotional contentment, do what is needed to have it.
• If you need more money, learn to earn, attract, and manage it.
• Whatever your real needs are, acquire the knowledge you need to have them satisfied and use it.

• Remember that you are in immortal spiritual being abiding in this world to awaken to the truth (the facts of life) and to live freely.

Grow to emotional maturity. Make wise choices. Be responsible for how you think, feel and behave. Don't dramatize fear, weakness, or small-minded attitudes and behaviors while hoping that God will deliver you from your self-created, restricted circumstances.

Come to terms with your memories. Forgive others if they have knowingly or unknowingly harmed you and forgive yourself for any past errors of judgment or behavior. Have clear intention and firm conviction that from this moment forward your experiences will always be in direct relationship to your clear states of awareness, rational mental states, and constructive behaviors. Established in Self- and God-knowledge, be enthusiastic.

Many people who are unhappy, and whose personal circumstances are oppressive or restricted, feel that they have little or no hope for improvement in the near or distant future. They may tend to observe situations as they are and be inclined to sink more deeply into thoughts and feelings of despair, try to find relief in useless social interactions, work hard or stay busy in an endeavor to take their attention off their problems, be superficially involved with spiritual practices and metaphysical studies, or abuse alcohol or drugs to dull their awareness and avoid self-responsible behaviors.

Addictive tendencies and other neurotic personality behaviors are symptoms of emotional discomfort or pain. Feelings of loneliness and insecurity are the result of thoughts and feelings of being alienated from God. Regardless of how earnestly a person endeavors to solve such problems by merely improving the human condition, the "cure" will only be temporary. It cannot result in total freedom from discomfort because the underlying cause will not have been directly confronted and completely eliminated.

LIFE CAN BE UNRESTRICTED AND ENJOYABLE

Because the universe is a manifestation of interactions of cosmic essences and forces emanated from God, there is nothing that can separate us from God. Because the amount of energy in the universe remains the same and is constantly changing from one form to another, there cannot be any lack in the universe. If we experience lack or limitation of any kind, it must be due to a deficiency of our understanding or our inappropriate actions or relationships.

Although we may not always know why we make mistakes, we can discover the cause and avoid making the same mistakes. If we are rightly resolved, there should be no sense of shame in regard to making mistakes. With diligent practice, we can soon learn to make only wise choices and to perform effective actions. The only person who never makes an error in judgement or behavior is the one who never tries to accomplish anything worthwhile.

Spiritual growth is in direct proportion to our ability to accept the good fortune that life can provide. During the past fifty years, during which I have met many thousands of people, I have never known of anyone with a habitual poverty consciousness who experienced an obvious degree of spiritual growth. I have known many such people who were pleasant, kind, and well-intentioned, and some who were able to generate a pleasant mood when praying or meditating. But real spiritual growth? No.

There are also many people who have good health, comfortable circumstances, and an abundance of material goods who have not yet experienced authentic spiritual growth. What prevents it is often more obvious: disinterest; egotism; pride of accomplishment; a rigid mental attitude; or tenacious mental and emotional attachment to their personality traits, status, relationships, or possessions.

It is not necessary, nor is it wise or practical, to renounce money, other useful material things, and meaningful relationships in order to be spiritually awake. What is needed is renunciation of mental and emotional attachment to things, concepts, feelings, behaviors, and relationships which are not of real value. Attachments keep attention, thoughts, and emotions fixated and confined. Detachment, along with insightful understanding, allows awareness to expand: to include everything that has real value and to discard nonessentials.

LEARN TO ATTRACT, HAVE, AND WISELY MANAGE MONEY AND OTHER NECESSARY RESOURCES

Many devotees of God who are healthy, well-educated, skillful, and have harmonious personal relationships, have difficulty having enough money to allow them to do the things they would like to do. They are not able to earn or attract surplus money or do not know how to manage it wisely when they have it. In most societies, because money is the commonly used medium of exchange for goods and services, it is necessary to have and use.

If you have difficulty in relating to or managing money, examine your thoughts and feelings about money. Do you think or feel that it is wrong for you to have money; you do not deserve it; it is not fair for you to have it when so many people do not; or that having and using it may cause you to become selfish and materialistic, interfere with your relationship with God, or prevent your spiritual growth? Does not having enough money provide you with a feeling of being superior to people who have it? Is it more important to be dysfunctional than to have the freedom to do things that an abundance of money might make possible? Are you more comfortable being restricted? Are you afraid of having to learn to be responsible for your thoughts, feelings, relationships, and actions? Do you secretly enjoy the limitations and problems that confine you? Do you prefer not to have enough money so that you can be like and have the companionship of your friends who also have financial restrictions? Has anyone ever told you that it is better not to have much money or that you would never accomplish anything worthwhile? Has your restricted lifestyle become so normal and habitual that you are reluctant to change it?

• When working or providing a service for which you will receive money, give value for value received. Ideally, the work you do or the service you perform should be enjoyable, in accord with your skills and abilities, and have entirely constructive effects.

• Don't spend money. To spend (Latin *expendere*, use up or consume) is to waste. Exchange the value that money represents for what you consider to be of value to you. Avoid buying nonessentials.

• Save a specific amount of what you have or earn. Invest it to earn more money for future use.

• On a regular schedule, freely yet thoughtfully give a portion of what you have or earn to responsible, well-managed endeavors which serve the public good and assist individuals in need.

• It is not necessary to tithe. A tithe is ten percent. Give less, or more, in accord with your financial circumstances and wisdom-guided choices. Give generously from your awareness of being prosperous and thankfully accept the abundance that life provides for you.

• Avoid the beggarly attitude of thinking that you can, or need to, bargain with God—that when you make a financial contribution to a worthy cause or volunteer your services you will receive in proportion to your giving or even an excess.

• Learn to be affluent: to always be in a continuous flow of resources and supportive events, circumstances and wholesome relationships for the highest good of yourself, others, the planet, and the universe.

• Transcend the idea of duality—the erroneous opinion that God is separate from the world.

ESTABLISHED IN CONSCIOUS AWARENESS OF WHOLENESS, LET LIFE FLOW FREELY THROUGH AND AROUND YOU

To avoid having your awareness contracted or confined when you are performing duties or relating to others, maintain your awareness of wholeness by faithfully adhering to a daily schedule of meditation practice and inspirational reading. When you become too extroverted, so physically or emotionally involved with activities and mundane circumstances that your inner peace is disturbed or your awareness of your relationship with God is blurred, withdraw for a while until you are soul-centered and God-aware. If, because of preoccupation with thoughts, memories, moods, or spiritual practices—or fear of or reluctance to relate to the world—you become so introverted that you are disinterested in performing your duties or functioning effectively, remind yourself of the importance of living a balanced life.

When you are apathetic or confused, do this:

• In a private place, sit quietly. Relax. Close your eyes or gaze into space without focusing on anything. Hold your eyes steady. Doing this will improve concentration and pacify thoughts and emotions.
• Disregard memories, moods, or problems.
• Soul-centered, watch and wait until you experience a spontaneous adjustment of viewpoint and your awareness is clear.
• Rest for several minutes, aware of the wholeness of life until you are peaceful, energetic, clear-minded, decisive, and purposeful.

Outgrow provincialism—the tendency to confine ideas, thoughts, activities, and relationships to a localized sphere of interest in order to continue to live in or maintain a small private world of traditional opinions, familiar circumstances, and habitual routines. If most of your thoughts and actions are focused only on surviving, satisfying personal desires, or getting through this incarnation with a minimum of discomfort, cultivate a more universal outlook.

Envision the possibilities available to you. Be receptive to learning about the world in which you live. Be curious. Learn, the principles by which its processes operate. Discover what you can do to live enjoyably and freely while helping others to be spiritually awake and freely functional. Be receptive to new ideas and to new, useful ways of doing things. Develop your powers of discriminative intelligence. Use your common sense. Be realistic and practical.

Just as the enlightened awareness of God-attuned souls blends with the collective consciousness of the planet's inhabitants and illumines it, the blurred awareness of unenlightened souls blends with the collective consciousness and clouds it. Impulses of God's grace which pervade planetary consciousness, and the clarified states of mind and awareness of spiritually aware human beings, nurture the well being of everyone and contribute to the orderly actions of nature. Your fully matured and actualized prosperity consciousness is of great value to you, others, and the universe.

Your life did not begin when you were physically born and will not end when the body dies. In truth, you were never born and you will never die. As a unit of God's being you were individualized, not created. At some point in time in the future, you will awaken completely from that illusional sense of Self-identity. Until then, you have much to learn, much good work to do, and much helpful service to render. You can do nothing for God because God is not other than you. All that occurs is God in action.

LESSON FOUR / PART THREE

MEDITATION PRACTICE

TECHNIQUE FOR MOVING AWARENESS THROUGH THE VITAL CENTERS

> By practice of kriya meditation, devotees unfold their full divinity and realize the perfection of God. Their entire being is illumined with the light of cosmic consciousness.
>
> – *Lahiri Mahasaya*

Attentive practice of this meditation technique will enable you to become familiar with the chakras, their qualities, and the states of awareness associated with them.

• Poised and alert, look into the spiritual eye. Bring your attention inward. Put your awareness with feeling-sensation inside the spinal pathway and brain. Feel the base chakra at the bottom of the spine. Contract the anal sphincter muscles once or twice to help locate the chakra. Withdraw your attention from externals. Listen in your ears to discern a subtle sound that might be present. Remain at that level for a few minutes.

• Bring your awareness and feeling-sensation upward to the second chakra at the sacrum region of the spine (the lower back). Gently flex the muscles in that region once or twice to help locate the chakra. Notice that your concentration is improving. If you hear a subtle inner sound, listen to it. Remain at that level for a few minutes.

• Bring your awareness and feeling-sensation upward to the third chakra in the middle of the back opposite the navel. Gently tense and relax the muscles in that region once or twice to help locate the chakra. If you hear a subtle inner sound, listen to it. Remain at that level for a few minutes.

• Bring your awareness and feeling-sensation upward to the fourth chakra between the shoulder blades. Press your shoulder blades together once or twice to help locate the chakra. If you hear a subtle sound, listen to it. Remain at that level for a few minutes. Withdraw your awareness from all subconscious influences and from thoughts and emotional states. Let any sense of personality dissolve.

• Bring your awareness and feeling-sensation upward to the fifth chakra in spine opposite the throat. Flex the muscles at the back of your neck once or twice to help locate the chakra. If you hear a subtle sound, listen to it. Remain at that level for a few minutes.

• Put your awareness and feeling-sensation into the spiritual eye. Look there. Elevate and spread your eyebrows two or three times, then be relaxed. If you hear a subtle sound, listen to it. If you are aware of inner light, let your attention be attracted it while listening to Om. Expand your awareness in Om, remembering its source. Give yourself completely to the inward flowing process.

• While still looking into the spiritual eye, also be aware and have feeling-sensation in the upper brain and outside of your head. Be aware only of your Self as pure, existence-being. Rest in that state of absorbed meditation for as long as it persists.

Use this technique during longer meditation sessions, after you have practiced a preliminary technique to elicit mental calmness and experienced the tranquil silence for a while. Because it culminates in listening to Om while contemplating the field of God, it can be used instead of the Primordial Sound meditation technique taught in the second lesson.

As you take your awareness upward through the seven chakras, you can progressively experience refined states of superconsciousness. At the fourth and fifth chakra stages, awareness may be somewhat clarified, with subtle thoughts and emotions still influential. At the spiritual eye, you may experience superconsciousness with the support of Om and inner light. At the seventh chakra level, you can realize oneness or wholeness without the support of any perceived object.

Regular practice of this method will greatly improve your powers of concentration, provide useful insights, enliven the chakras, gently encourage the awakening of kundalini energies, and enable you to acquire conscious control of your states of awareness.

Do not be preoccupied with subjective perceptions or allow impatience to erode your inner peace. After meditation, remain aware of your relationship with the Infinite as you consciously live your life with meaningful purpose. Now devoted to the enlightenment path, you are on the right course in life. Adhere to it. Evidence of authentic spiritual growth will be increasingly apparent as your soul qualities emerge, your awareness is clarified, and your functional abilities improve. The only worthwhile test of the usefulness of this way of life and these methods is your personal experience.

Note: Practice the meditation techniques described in these lessons privately or with others who have learned them from these lessons or from a qualified kriya yoga meditation teacher. Please do not teach them to your friends who are curious or because you want to help them. Individuals who are sincerely interested can be informed about these lessons or be referred to a qualified teacher. They can then learn and practice with benefit.

> When samadhi [superconsciousness] without mental
> transformations is unwavering, the meditator's awareness
> reflects the reality of pure consciousness.
> – *Patanjali's yoga-sutras 1:43*

HOW TO USE AFFIRMATIONS EFFECTIVELY

When necessary, use affirmations to arouse your soul forces and clarify your perceptions. Don't use them in an endeavor to program or further condition the mind. Speak a selected affirmation aloud two or three times with conviction. Quietly speak it two or three times. Whisper it a few times. Mentally speak it. Cease speaking. Experience it superconsciously.

A free-flowing current of inspiration energizes and illumines my mind, purifies my intellect, unveils my intuition, enlivens my body, and empowers my wisely chosen, skillfully performed actions.

I am always fully awake to the truth of my Being and my relationship to the Infinite. Because I remain in tune with the rhythms of life, my constructive desires are always easily fulfilled and I am always in the flow of good fortune.

Consciously established in vivid awareness of my true nature, knowing that I am included in the wholeness of the infinite field of Consciousness, sustaining my vision of ideal possibilities, I use my mind, energies, resources, and functional abilities wisely and creatively.

I enjoy learning and I learn easily. I am keenly interested in the skillful application of my innate knowledge that unfolds and the practical knowledge that I acquire. As my knowledge increases and my skills improve, my awareness expands and I am increasingly competent and successful.

I willingly participate with life's unfolding processes, live with firm resolve, attend to necessary duties, perform effective actions, and meditate regularly. Anchored in the Infinite, I am peaceful, productive, and successful.

It is easy to live by faith. I know that I abide in the boundless field of Infinite Consciousness from which the universe is emanated and by which it is nurtured. I know that what I clearly visualize and firmly believe to be true, I can definitely experience.

I am prosperous. I live effectively. I am receptive to all of the unplanned good fortune that the universe provides. I am always responsive to the freely expressive actions of God's enlivening, nurturing, and supportive grace.

The reality of the Presence of God of which I am consciously aware is the inexhaustible Source of the continuous flow of resources and events that are always provided for my complete well-being and highest good.

REVIEW OF LESSON FOUR

1. What are the four characteristics of a soul completely identified with primordial nature and its manifestations?

    1 _____ 2 _____

    3 _____ 4 _____

2. List the five aspects of prana which are expressive in the physical body.

    1 _____

    2 _____

    3 _____

    4 _____

    5 _____

3. Define *kundalini*. _____

4. Where are the seven chakras located:

    1 _____ 2 _____

    3 _____ 4 _____

    5 _____ 6 _____

    7 _____

5. Review the characteristics associated with the chakras. Feel where the chakras are located in your spine and brain. When you sit to meditate, put your awareness in the spine, then elevate it to the spiritual eye and crown chakra when you listen to your mantra or abide in the silence.

6. Practice the basic pranayama routine described on page 69. Use it just before you meditate or whenever you want calm the body or clarify your thought processes.

PERSONAL APPLICATION

1. Cultivate a consciousness (awareness) of being prosperous in all aspects of your life. Learn to always be in the flow of resources and supportive events and relationships for your highest good.

2. What are some indications of prosperity?

    _____

    _____

    _____

    _____

3. Write a clearly defined list of your needs. Know that the universe can satisfy them.

    _____

    _____

    _____

    _____

4. Learn to attract and wisely manage money. Exchange the value that it represents for what you want or need.

5. When you are tired or confused, practice the procedure described on page 74.

6. Be a possibility-thinker. Imagine what can be possible for you and claim it for yourself. Be sure to "see" yourself spiritually enlightened.

7. Practice the meditation technique to move your awareness through the chakras.

8. Speak aloud the affirmations on page 77. Do this with conviction.

9. You are an immortal, spiritual being. Live in accord with that knowledge.

THE WISDOM OF THE YOGA-SUTRAS

The superior, constructive influence of [superconscious] samadhi eliminates restrictive subliminal tendencies and instinctual driving forces.

The tranquil flow of awareness then occurs due to its innate purity.

Because of the [constructive] influence of samadhi, fluctuations of mental modifications cease and awareness of wholeness prevails.

When the meditator's concentration is completely focused, sequential ideas that arise in the mind are similar.

The preceding four verses explain the kinds, fine varieties, and states of transformations that occur in the meditator's field of awareness. *– 3:9–13*

Mental, moral, and spiritual strength are acquired by contemplation on friendliness, compassion, and other noble qualities. By contemplation on various aspects of power, one becomes empowered. By contemplation on the light of Consciousness, intuitive knowledge of veiled, subtle, and remote things is acquired. *– 3:24–26*

By contemplation on absolute pure Consciousness, all innate knowledge is revealed.

By contemplation on the heart [Consciousness], knowledge [of it] is realized.

By contemplation on the self-existent reality of Consciousness, one acquires the ability to clearly discern the difference between it and ordinary states of awareness.

By contemplation on the reality of God, exceptional powers of perception are acquired.

If allowed to flow outwardly, these powers become obstacles to spiritual growth and to perfecting samadhi. If used wisely, they become superior abilities used to resist, weaken, and eliminate subliminal influences which restrict free flows of awareness. *– 3:33–38*

By contemplation on the senses, their powers of cognition and inherent characteristics, pervasiveness, and influences, mastery of them is acquired.

By meditative contemplation on the distinction between the attributes of nature and the reality of one Consciousness, perceptions of omnipotence and omniscience are acquired.

When the causes of bondage have been removed by renouncing attachments to superior abilities and to perceptions of omnipotence and omnipresence, the soul is liberated.

Upon awakening to Self-knowledge, there should be no pride in regard to [one's] spiritual status or attachment to it, as this can cause a return to former, unclear states of awareness.

– 3:48-52

Absolute discriminative knowledge is simultaneous knowledge of the entirety of the universe and its aspects and manifestations.

When the purity of individualized awareness is the same as the purity of the Self, [then] absolute liberation of consciousness is realized. *– 3:55,56*

LESSON FIVE

PHILOSOPHY

THE FUNDAMENTALS OF YOGA PRACTICE

The brain and spinal pathway is considered to be the seat of consciousness in the body. Moving life force through the chakras is the kriya pranayama that purifies the mind and results in happiness. Thus purifying the mind and physical systems, the truth seeker attains a state of beatitude.   – *Sri Yukteswar*

The systematic procedures used to clarify awareness and restore it to wholeness which comprise the practices of yoga were discovered thousands of years ago by revelation and experimentation. Because the philosophical principles and practices of yoga emerged in India where Hinduism is dominant, many people erroneously presume yoga to be an aspect of that religious tradition. Yoga can be, and is, practiced by devotees of God of various religious traditions as well as by those with no formal affiliation. It has been the testimony of yogis that, if one begins yoga practice without having a concept of God, the reality of God is eventually apprehended.

To be of value, yogic practices should be compatible with one's psychological temperament, capacity to learn, and ability to practice.

• <u>*Hatha Yoga* routines enable the practitioner to acquire mastery over physical and psychological states by skillful application of specific postures (*asanas*); pranayama; techniques to stimulate and control flows of life force (*mudras*); and meditation.</u> When the sun (*ha*) and moon (*tha*) currents of life force in the spine, and their influences, are harmonized, mental and emotional fluctuations cease, concentration is undisturbed, and superconscious states can easily emerge. It is best to practice hatha yoga routines in a meditative mood, without strain or force. While the physical results—improvement of muscle strength, flexibility, blood and lymph circulation, and hormonal secretions—are beneficial, the primary purpose of practice is to nurture physical and psychological well-being so that vital forces can flow freely and superconscious meditation can be practiced effectively.

If hatha yoga routines are learned by participating in classes, when proficiency is acquired practice can be done privately without the social support of others. In recent years, hatha yoga has been highly publicized and aggressively marketed. While this undoubtedly has some value in that it benefits many people at a superficial level and helps to make yoga practice acceptable to the general public, the commercialization and competitiveness that sometimes results is contrary to the ideals and purposes of the traditions of yoga. For the ordinary person, extensive learning and practice of hatha yoga is not necessary. Practice of a few basic procedures is sufficient.

Preoccupation with the physical practices may contract and confine awareness rather than clarify and expand it. When a spiritually advanced disciple asked Paramahansaji if he should intensify his hatha yoga practice, the response was, "No, you may lose your bliss." Explanation: If attention is allowed to become fascinated with physical routines, one may be inclined to neglect the cultivation of Self- and God-realization.

• *Bhakti yoga* is the devotional, reverential, surrendered approach to apprehending the reality of God by acknowledging the innate, divine nature of everyone and everything and renouncing the illusional sense of independent Selfhood. If your aspiration to enlightenment is impelling, any kind of ritual worship that may performed, while perhaps useful at the early stages of spiritual growth, will eventually be replaced by interior contemplation and superconscious perceptions which will result in non-dependence upon modes of worship and transcendence of external and internal objects of devotion. It is best if a devotional temperament is stabilized by emotional maturity and balanced by intellectual development. Dramatization of emotionalism or irrational behaviors is not useful.

• *Karma yoga* is the way of mental and emotional renunciation of the results of actions, rather than the avoidance of the performance of necessary actions. A devotee of God is counseled to fulfill duties and perform actions cheerfully and skillfully without attachment to either the actions or the results. There should be no desire to be praised for one's actions, nor should one who is rightly resolved react to blame or criticism. Thoughts and actions should be wholesome and constructive. We are participants in the drama of life, in this world to learn to live in accord with the laws of consciousness, mind, and nature and to cooperate with the Power that enlivens and maintains the orderly processes of the universe. Constructive, selfless service purifies the ego, fosters humility (absence of arrogance), and weakens and neutralizes karma (subconscious conditionings).

• *Jnana* (GYA-na) *yoga* is the way of developing and wisely using purified powers of discriminative intelligence to discern the truth of Self, God, and the universe, and learning to accurately perceive the relationships between causes and effects that relate to everyday life. In this way, delusions are eliminated and illusions cease. A devotee of God is advised to inquire, "What am I?", "What is God?", "How is the universe produced and maintained?" Intellectual inquiry should be balanced by devotion, selflessness, and meditation practice. The intellect can enable one to apprehend the processes of Consciousness; comprehension (realization) is the result of direct perception which does not require the use of the mind or intellect.

• *Raja* (royal, regal) *yoga* practice includes the most useful aspects of all of the systems of yoga, with emphasis on proficient meditation and mastery of states of consciousness. An integrated approach to total well-being and functional living which facilitates rapid spiritual growth, it is the most beneficial spiritual path.

The eightfold raja yoga way of liberation of consciousness:

1. Five external disciplines: restraints (*yamas*). The resisting and mastery of harmful impulses and habits by choice, will power, and replacing them with the opposite characteristics of: harmlessness; truthfulness; honesty; conservation and transformation of vital forces; and renunciation of attachments which makes possible appropriate relationships and prudent use of available resources.

2. Five internal disciplines: not-restraints (*niyamas*). Physical and environmental cleanliness and mental purity; the cultivation of soul contentment in all circumstances; attitude and behavioral modification to effect psychological transformation; Self-analysis, metaphysical study, and meditative contemplation to apprehend one's true essence and the reality of God; and compliant surrender of the illusional sense of selfhood in favor of awakening to awareness and realization of transcendent realities.

The external and internal practices remove obstructions to the soul's inclination to be expressive and provide the foundation for effective and progressive authentic spiritual growth.

3. Meditation posture (*asana*). A poised, upright, seated posture which can easily be maintained so that attention can be devoted to the practice of meditation and meditative contemplation.

4. Life forces flowing freely and harmoniously (*pranayama*), which may spontaneously occur or be encouraged by breath regulation.

5. Internalization of attention (*pratyhara*), when awareness is detached from the senses and directed inward. Concentrated attention, devotion, looking into the spiritual eye, and bringing life forces upward through the chakras are some of the means by which this stage can be quickly accomplished.

6. Concentration (*dharana*). A focused flow of attention.

7. Meditation (*dhyana*). Unwavering concentration.

8. Superconsciousness (*samadhi*).

Other names, such as *kriya yoga* (the intentional performance of constructive actions and special meditation techniques), *laya yoga* (absorption of awareness in Om), and *kundalini yoga* (awakening of dormant soul forces and allowing them to flow upward to the higher brain) are used to indicate specialized practices.

If yoga practice is to be effective, a radical adjustment of viewpoint and behavior is usually necessary. Egocentric mental attitudes can be replaced with a more cosmic outlook. Emotion-driven behaviors can be replaced with dispassionate, thoughtful, attentive performance of appropriate actions. Erroneous opinions about God, life, and death can be replaced with intellectual understanding that will, in time, be replaced with flawless apprehension and experience (realization) of what is true. Ordinary self-conscious life is often compelled by subliminal tendencies and confused choices. The soul-centered life is spontaneously expressive and wisdom-directed.

If emotional maturity is lacking, the novice devotee may easily be inclined to escape into fantasy, to see mystery where there is none, or to imagine a relationship with God or saints which is not realistic. For the rational devotee, yoga practice will be acknowledged for what it is: a practical means by which psychological transformation can quickly be effected and authentic spiritual growth can be facilitated.

Information about yoga can be acquired from books and teachers; accurate knowledge of yoga can only be acquired by experimentation which provides personal experience.

During my first private talk with Paramahansa Yogananda, he advised me to read his books and a few others that he recommended, to practice meditation on a regular schedule, and cultivate awareness of the presence of God at all times. On another occasion, he told me, "Dive deep into the ocean of God when you meditate. In a year or two, your powers of discernment will be so well-developed that you will be able to tell the difference between truth and untruth."

The kriya yoga path, which integrates the most useful practices of all of the systems of yoga, is effective only when it is actualized to the utmost of one's ability. Superficial interest in awakening to Self-realization and inattentive adherence to recommended lifestyle regimens and meditation practices will not result in peace of mind or satisfying spiritual growth.

If you do what you need to do to, you *can* be fully Self- and God-realized in this incarnation. Believe it! Aspire to it! Diligently apply your knowledge, skills, and innate resources!

Although individualized fields of awareness [souls] and their activities are diverse, one Cosmic Field of Awareness originates them.
– *Patanjali's yoga-sutras 4:5*

VITALIZING THE PHYSICAL BODY

Before traveling from India to America, in 1920, Paramahansa Yogananda innovated a routine for vitalizing the physical body which he later taught to many thousands of his students in America. He said that soul force flowing into the body through the medulla oblongata at the base of the brain could be consciously directed by visualization and will. Experiment with these "energization" routines. Do them daily for at least three weeks to become familiar with them and experience benefits. It can be helpful to do them before meditating or whenever you want to reduce stress and feel enlivened.

To practice: with attention at the spiritual eye center, when you gently tense a muscle (only for a moment), imagine and feel life force flowing to it from the medulla center. When you relax the muscle, feel life force withdrawing from it.

1. Stand upright, relaxed and poised. In the following sequence, gently and quickly tense the muscles and attract life force to them, then relax and let the life force withdraw.

    Back, front, and sides of neck. Upper back. Upper chest. Upper arms. Forearms. Upper stomach. Abdomen. Right and left buttocks. Right and left lower legs. Feet.

2. Stand upright. Bend your knees slightly. Extend your arms to the front, palms together. Close your hands into a fist. While inhaling deeply, mildly tense the muscles of the body from your feet to your neck in a wavelike movement, spreading your arms as you inhale and feeling the body to be vitalized. Exhale and relax while returning to the starting position. Do this two or three times. Inhale through your nostrils. Exhale through your mouth. As you inhale and mildly tense your muscles, with awareness at the spiritual eye and medulla, attract life force into your body. Let the energy withdraw from your muscles as you relax.

3. To strengthen the vocal cords. Roll your tongue back and forth a few times. Pull it back toward the throat and push it forward. Relax. Drop your head forward. Mildly tense the front of the neck, hold the tension, slowly lift your head. Relax. Do this twice.

4. To increase digestive powers and awaken life forces in the lower spine. Stand up. Bend forward with your hands on your knees, knees slightly bent. Inhale. Exhale. Restrain the breath. Gently press your chin against the upper chest. Elevate the rib cage and lift the muscles of the abdomen upward and inward toward the spine. Relax and exhale. Maintaining the position, let your breathing be restored to its normal rate. Repeat two or three times. (This procedure is described in hatha yoga texts: *uddiyana*, upward movement; *bandha*, lock.) In this instance the "lock" at the throat restrains the breath.

Affirmation to be Used Before Doing Your Vitalization Routine
O Eternal Energy! Awaken within me conscious will, conscious vitality, conscious health.
Good will to all. Vitality to all. Health to all.
– Paramahansa Yogananda

LIFESTYLE GUIDELINES

THE SCIENCE OF SELF- AND GOD-REALIZATION

Self-realization is knowing in body, mind, and soul that you are wholly established in God. To be Self-realized, you only have to improve your knowing. To be God-realized is to know your [true] Self as the great ocean of Spirit by dissolving the delusion that you are this little ego, body, and personality.

– *Paramahansa Yogananda*

science Latin *scire*, to know (by observation, identification, description, and experimental investigation).

Self- and God-realization that result in soul liberation should be the purpose of yoga practice. Not all practitioners of yoga aspire to liberation of consciousness. They only desire the psychological or physical benefits, or an adjustment in viewpoint or improvement in functional abilities that will enable them to live comfortably and effectively. Their priorities are related to their mundane concerns: survival, being reasonably free from pain or difficulties, acquiring material things, having compatible personal relationships, and sense enjoyments.

Even without strong aspiration to be Self-realized, if one lives a wholesome, conflict-free life and meditates on a regular schedule to the stage of superconsciousness, spiritual growth will slowly occur. It will occur much faster when aspiration to be enlightened is constant. Such aspiration awakens dormant soul forces, attracts a supportive response from Cosmic Mind, and attunes the devotee's mind and awareness with refined levels of Consciousness. The always-present impulses of grace can then more easily be influential.

THE DIRECT WAY TO AWAKEN
TO SELF- AND GOD-REALIZATION

If you sincerely aspire to be Self-realized, do not allow anyone or any circumstance to distract you from your primary purpose. Do not ask anyone for their opinion regarding the possibility of your being able to awaken from the "dream of mortality" to full realization of your true nature and the reality of God. Do not think that you must struggle for several incarnations to overcome karma or have your awareness restored to wholeness. You have complete knowledge of the wholeness of life and all of its processes within you. It has only to be acknowledged and unveiled.

Use your powers of discriminative intelligence to discern the difference between your pure-conscious essence of being and the fragmented states of mind and awareness which are characteristic of ordinary self-conscious (personality-identified) states. If you are unable to immediately do this, you will at least have fleeting perceptions of what is true and permanent in contrast to what is illusory and temporary. If you are aware of inner resistance to being Self-realized, analyze and eliminate the problem:

• Are you afraid to be Self-realized?
• Are you afraid to comprehend and experience the reality of God as God is?
• Are you concerned about how your life might be changed when you are more spiritually awake?
• Are you afraid of what others might think of you when you are spiritually enlightened?
• Are your circumstances, whether pleasant or unpleasant, so comfortable that you are resistant to change of any kind?
• Do you regard Self- and God-realization as a desirable state to be eventually experienced, but not now?
• Do you consider being able to clearly apprehend your true nature and the reality of God to be like "a pearl of great price" for which you would gladly exchange anything to have?

Self-realization cannot be earned or obtained. It is available to anyone who is willing and able to allow it to replace the habitual, egocentric state, the illusional sense of Self-identity which is the primary cause of irrational thinking, dysfunctional behaviors, and most of the suffering and misfortune that individuals may experience.

The major obstacle to spiritual awakening is lack of sincere desire to experience it. If you say that you desire to apprehend and experience your true nature and the reality of God, what are you doing to allow yourself to do it?

• Do you maintain an optimistic mental attitude?
• Do you nurture your physical health with sufficient rest, adequate exercise, and nutritious food?
• Are you self-confident, self-reliant, and emotionally mature?
• Do you perform your duties skillfully?
• Do you choose your friends and social companions wisely?
• Is your choice of metaphysical reading material of real value?
• Do you remember to perceive and acknowledge the innate, divine nature of everyone and everything?
• Do you meditate on a regular schedule to the stage of alert, tranquil, superconscious awareness, rather than for the purpose of experiencing a pleasant mood?

Awakening to Self- and God-realization will not remove you from this world; it will enable you to know yourself as you are and the world for what it is. You will know that you are an aspect of God's being and that the world is a manifestation of cosmic forces emanated from God.

Karma (subconscious conditionings) will be weakened, dissolved, and transcended. Your pure, soul qualities will be effortlessly expressed. Exceptional powers of perception will be unveiled. Functional skills will be greatly improved. You will be able to live effectively without restrictions, fully aware of your constructive role as a willing participant in the drama of cosmic life.

Spiritual growth is not determined by gender, personal history or circumstances, or social or financial status. The determining factors are 1) ardent desire to be enlightened and 2) effective performance of necessary actions—attitude and behavior modification and useful spiritual practices. Unwavering desire to be enlightened keeps attention focused on your purpose. Effective actions remove mental, emotional, and physical obstacles, improve intellectual and intuitive powers, and allow innate knowledge to emerge and blossom.

The soul qualities described in the first three verses of chapter sixteen of the Bhagavad Gita are naturally expressed by enlightened people:

> Fearlessness, devotion, purity of heart, abiding in yoga [samadhi] and having right knowledge, charitable giving, self-restraint, holy offerings, study of sacred texts, austerity, and uprightness; nonviolence, truthfulness, absence of anger, renunciation, serenity, freedom from finding fault, compassion for all beings, absence of cravings, gentleness, modesty, steadiness; vigor, forgiveness, fortitude, freedom from malice and pride are the divine endowments.

If you do not yet spontaneously express them, their cultivation will be helpful spiritual practice which will purify your mind, clarify your awareness, make your life more comfortable and meaningful, be of benefit to others, and enable you to more easily awaken to Self- and God-realization.

Realization is accurate apprehension and actual experience. If you have had glimpses of your true nature, continue to contemplate the essence of your being and the reality of God until your realization is permanent. If you are already Self-realized, continue with spiritual practices until your mind and awareness is completely purified. If you are not yet Self-realized, be firmly resolved to be spiritually awake as quickly as possible. Do these things:

• After meditation practice, or anytime when you are alone and quiet, inquire into what you are at the innermost level of your being. You are not the mind which is subject to being modified. You are not your moods which are changeable. You are not your personality, the "mask" you wear to present yourself to others. You are not your body which was born and will cease to exist. Through the years, although your mind, emotional states, personality characteristics, and physical body have changed, you have not changed. What is the essence of your being which observes, perceives, determines, and experiences, yet does not change?

• Meditate every day to the stage of alert, tranquil awareness. Rest there for a little while, then go more deeply into the silence. Contemplate God, the one field of Consciousness. Contemplate the field of pure, existence-being which is identical with the essence of your being. Let your remaining sense of independent selfhood dissolve in oneness.

• Live in accord with your highest understanding: soul-centered, devoted to learning, spiritual awakening, and selfless service until you are fully enlightened. When you are fully enlightened, all of your thoughts and actions will be spontaneously appropriate.

Often, the most difficult adjustment of attitude to make is that of learning to perceive ourselves as spiritual beings in relationship to our mental states, emotions, physical body, and circumstances rather than thinking and feeling that we are limited human beings with aspirations to become Self- and God-realized.

When a soul's awareness is blurred and confused, it is inclined to identify with mental and emotional states, the physical body and the senses, and environmental circumstances. When identification with external conditions (including thoughts, memories, and emotions which are also external to the soul) is habitual, awareness is confined, the intellect is clouded, and intuition is suppressed. The solution to this problem is to discern the difference between soul awareness and that which is perceived, and to detach attention from external circumstances by practicing superconscious meditation.

Meditative superconscious perceptions provide actual experience of being other than mental attributes or a body and its sensations. When not meditating, harmoniously integrate superconscious awareness with thoughts, emotions, and physical sensations. This can most easily be done by being soul-centered and discerning.

As with any science, the reliable means by which Self- and God-realization can be actualized have to be examined, analyzed, defined, and applied. Attentive, experimental application of these methods will result in personal experiences which will verify them.

> Better than rulership over all the world, better than going
> to heaven, is the reward of the first step in holiness.
> – *The Dhammapada (dharma path*

MEDITATION PRACTICE

THE "PATH OF GOD" TECHNIQUE

> Within every person is the subtle path of God-realization. When one's awareness is completely established in this path, prana flows therein in rhythmic radiance. This [procedure] is known by yogis as divine breathing. Regular practice results in complete spiritual transformation. — *Lahiri Mahasaya*

This technique is especially helpful to spiritual aspirants who are able to comprehend its value and will regularly use it to deepen and enrich their meditation experience.

• Sit upright. Relax. Look into the spiritual eye. Be aware of and *feel* your spine. Visualize it as a hollow tube extending from the bottom of the spine to the top of your head.

• Partially open your mouth. Inhale. Exhale. Mildly constrict the throat and inhale in through your mouth, creating a mild suction effect in the throat. Feel the cool sensation of the air in your throat as you do this. Relate the cool sensation to your spine and feel that you are gently pulling a cool current upward through it. (After acquiring proficiency, breathe through the nostrils with the mouth closed.)

• At the end of inhalation, with the current of life force in the head, pause for a moment.

• Exhale slowly and naturally through your mouth and feel a warm, soothing current descending through the spine. Pause for a moment. Repeat the process.

• Continue this practice until you are inclined to disregard it and rest in the tranquil silence.

Inhalation is medium-slow and deeper than usual. Breathe from the diaphragm in the normal way without excessive expansion or contraction of the rib cage. The usual rate of breathing when the body is at rest is 15 to 18 times a minute. When using this technique, breathing is slower because it is deeper and longer than usual. Practice patiently until you are able to feel a current of life force ascending and descending through the spine as you inhale and exhale. Visualization is not as important as feeling. The ascending current provides a joyous or pleasurable sensation; the descending current is warm and soothing. Except for the momentary pauses after inhalation and exhalation, breathing is gentle yet intentional, effortless, smooth, and continuous.

This practice neutralizes the influences of *prana* (which regulates inhalation) and *apana* (which regulates exhalation). As you become more relaxed and inwardly focused (simultaneously aware of the spine, spiritual eye, and brain) notice that your breathing is slower and more refined. Cultivate awareness of the current moving up and down in the spine, as though breathing through it.

The ascending and descending currents of life force magnetize the spine, encourage gentle awakening of dormant energies in the body, and enliven the chakras. The beneficial, satisfying results are mental and emotional calmness and soul-centered awareness that prevails during and after practice of this procedure.

This method of acquiring conscious control over mental states and states of awareness is mentioned in the Bhagavad Gita. In the following verses, the word *yoga* is used to refer to both the practice of meditation and to samadhi, the culmination of practice:

> Some practitioners, by offering apana into prana and prana into apana, harmonize and neutralize their actions. – *4:29*

> The devotee who is continually self-disciplined, with mental impulses subdued and tranquil, realizes the supreme state of oneness (samadhi). – *6:15*

> As a lamp in a windless place does not flicker, such is the concentration of the meditator who, with mental impulses subdued, practices yoga. With mental processes restrained [pacified and stilled] by yoga practice and content in Self-knowledge, the meditator experiences infinite happiness which is apprehended by the intellect and transcends the senses, and there established, does not waver from the truth. – *6:19-21*

> Abandoning all egocentric desires, subduing the senses, the meditator should gradually become still. With the intellect firmly concentrated on the reality of the true Self, let nothing else be thought about or contemplated.
> Whenever mental processes fluctuate and attention wavers, they should be restrained by self-determination.
> That practitioner of yoga whose mind is peaceful and whose emotions are calm, whose awareness is purified and who is God-realized, awakens to the highest bliss.
> Thus constantly practicing yoga, the devotee freed from all restraints easily has knowledge and experience of God that bestows boundless happiness. – *6:24-28*

"Boundless happiness" is the sheer joy of Self- and God-realization that permanently removes awareness from all restraints of ignorance, delusions, and illusions.

> When fluctuations in the field of individualized awareness cease,
> the seer [the Self which perceives] abides in its true nature.
> – *Patanjali's yoga sutras 1:3*

REVIEW OF LESSON FIVE

1. List the five basic yoga systems and the emphasis of each of them.

    1 _____

    2 _____

    3 _____

    4 _____

    5 _____

2. What are the eight stages of raja yoga practice?

    1 _____   2 _____

    3 _____   4 _____

    5 _____   5 _____

    7 _____   8 _____

3. What are the five external disciplines? Endeavor to actualize them.

    1 _____   2 _____

    3 _____   4 _____

    5 _____

4. What are the five internal disciplines? Endeavor to actualize them.

    1 _____   2 _____

    3 _____   4 _____

    5 _____

5. Define Self-realization.

    _____

PERSONAL APPLICATION

1. Aspire to be Self- and God-realized.

2. Review the questions on page 87 and honestly answer them.

3. What are two factors which determine spiritual growth?

   _____

   _____

4. What are some of the soul qualities which are spontaneously expressed by one who is enlightened? Nurture and express these qualities.

   _____

   _____

   _____

   _____

5. Develop your powers of discriminative intelligence. Discern the difference between the essence of your being, which is pure consciousness, and your thoughts, moods, and physical sensations. Established in Self-awareness, think rationally and act wisely.

6. If you have been meditating for at least six months, include the "path of God" technique in your daily meditation routine. Do it gently. Feel the current of life force flow up when you breathe in and flow down when you breathe out. After concluding the practice of this, or any meditation technique, sit in the tranquil silence. Let any remaining sense of illusional selfhood dissolve. Meditate *in* God.

7. Once a week, twice a month, or once a month, meditate longer and more deeply than you usually do. Use the meditation techniques of your choice until your mind is peaceful, then sit in the deep silence. When you sit longer, your innate impulse to have your awareness restored to wholeness will determine your meditation experience. Adjustments of states of awareness will occur spontaneously. Your awareness will be clarified. Refined states of superconsciousness will be experienced.

8. After meditation practice, retain your calm state. As superconscious influences blend with ordinary states of awareness, cosmic consciousness will emerge. You will perceive yourself to be one with the omnipresent field of Consciousness.

LIGHT ON THE PATH

The following verses are from the *Shiva Samhita*, written over five centuries ago. The author is unknown. The word *Shiva* represents the field of absolute pure Consciousness, the repository of all knowledge. A *samhita* (Sanskrit, "to place together") is a collected body of knowledge. In this treatise, the core emphasis is *yoga*; with philosophical concepts and explanations of principles and practices presented in five chapters of 212 verses. It is assumed that the reader of the text has the help of a teacher to explain its meaning or has sufficient powers of intellectual and intuitive discernment to understand it.

Sitting in a meditation posture, the yogi should focus attention inward to the spiritual eye. By successful accomplishment, one experiences unqualified, pure happiness, therefore, this should be done with concentrated endeavor.

One who thus practices obtains mastery of prana in a short duration of time. The prana then enters the middle channel [in the spine]. One who practices this with diligence experiences the unfoldment of exceptional powers of perception and can explore the three worlds [physical, astral, and subtle realms] at will.

When the [meditating] yogi is constantly aware of the spiritual eye, fire like lighting is perceived there. By contemplating this light, the mind is purified and karma is removed.

The awareness of one who contemplates the field of pure consciousness then becomes absorbed in it. The yogi desirous of success should obtain this knowledge. By habitual practice one becomes Self- and God-realized.

Having mastered all the elements and being devoid of all hopes and worldly connections, when the yogi meditates on the spiritual eye, mental processes are pacified and the siddhi [unrestricted soul ability] of being free in space unfolds.

The accomplished yogi perceives light. By concentrated practice on it one becomes the lord of the light [obtains success in working with that light].

The two-petaled [with dual currents of prana] chakra is between the eyebrows.

Within it, is the eternal *bija* [seed essence], brilliant as a full moon. The wise devotee who knows [experiences] this light is never distracted from the path. By contemplation on this light, one obtains the highest success.

The space between *ida* and *pingala* is the holy abode of divinity. There, it is said, the Lord of the universe dwells. The greatness of this holy place has been declared in many scriptures by truth-perceiving sages; its secret has been eloquently expounded by them.

Sushumna nadi in the spine extends to the *Brahmarandhra* ["*God*-opening," the soft spot at the top of the skull]. The lotus [chakra] there is *sahasrara* [thousand petaled]. In it dwells brilliant, white light. From it, elixir (the fluid of immortality) is continually exuding.

LESSON SIX

PHILOSOPHY

AWAKENING THE INNER POTENTIAL

The light of God shines at the spiritual eye, the inner door
that leads the soul's awareness into the realm of divine glory of
God. The reality of God that dwells in each person can be known
by entering the sanctuary of illumined consciousness.
– Lahiri Mahasaya

In the body of a person who is not spiritually awake, surplus soul force
which is not needed to maintain physical functions remains dormant
at the base chakras. *Kundalini* is the "coiled" dormant soul force with
innate potential to be expressive and transformative. It is an individualized aspect of the power of Consciousness which pervades the
universe. Its energy (*shakti*) is an individualized aspect of the cosmic
energy that enlivens nature.

Kundalini awakens naturally when the soul's innate urge to have
its awareness clarified and restored to wholeness is dominant. It can
be encouraged to awaken by sustained aspiration to be spiritually
aware, devotion, compassion, prayer, pranayama practice, practice of
certain hatha yoga routines, the use of mantras and other meditation
techniques, and superconscious meditation practice. It can awaken
spontaneously when psychological and physical health is optimum,
when one is in an environment where refined spiritual forces prevail,
and when the mind and nervous system are receptive in the presence
of a person in whom kundalini energies are freely flowing.

When the activation of a disciple's vital forces occurs because of
the influence of the guru's kundalini energy, the process of energy transmission is referred to as *shaktipat*. When the disciple is receptive, the
transmission may occur spontaneously or it may be induced by the
guru's intention, touch, or eye contact.

Receptivity to the beneficial influences of the guru's consciousness
and awakened spiritual energies can be improved by regular meditation practice and by nurturing faith, mental and emotional calmness,
and humility. Egocentricity should be renounced; mental calmness
should be maintained; psychological conflicts should be resolved; aspiration to be Self-realized should be fervent.

I experienced a sudden and unexpected awakening of kundalini
energies a few weeks after I met Paramahansa Yogananda. He had not
suggested that it would occur, nor did he ask me about my reactions. In
the weeks that followed, he quietly observed me and, from time to time,
provided helpful advice of a personal nature.

Unlike the indiscriminate publishing of information (much of which is unworthy of being called knowledge) about spiritual growth processes in our current Era, enlightened teachers emphasize the superior value of personal instruction. The qualified (well-prepared) disciple can then acquire accurate information and be guided through progressive stages of psychological and spiritual growth.

Awakened kundalini energies flow upward through the chakras, enlivening their actions. The mind is energized. The body is vitalized. Psychological transformation may be gradual or fast. Awareness is clarified and, no longer confined, expands. Powers of discriminative intelligence are enhanced. Intuitive powers improve. Superconscious states emerge. Interest in ordinary activities and relationships may diminish. If the devotee's attention and actions are not engaged in purposeful endeavors, confusion may be experienced. For this reason, when undergoing adjustments of states of awareness, it is important to adhere to routines of orderly living and meditation practice which will contribute to mental and emotional stability. It is also helpful to obtain sufficient sleep and choose nourishing foods.

Avoid late-night activities, excessive socializing, and fasting from food, all of which may aggravate vata characteristics and contribute to irrational thinking or fantasies. Avoid anxiety about the outcome of your transformative experiences.

Don't discuss your subjective experiences with anyone except your guru or a qualified mentor. Avoid allowing your awareness to become confined and restricted because of preoccupation with yourself.

There is no need to fear the awakening of your own energies. Live a balanced life and let natural spiritual growth occur. During the fifty years (as of this writing) that I have practiced yoga, traveled to many countries, and interacted with thousands of people, I have never met anyone who experienced severe physical discomfort or disabling psychological problems which were caused by kundalini energies.

The few people I have met (or heard about) who attributed their physical, mental, or emotional discomfort to kundalini awakening were misinformed when reading a book or magazine article, someone incorrectly advised them, or they were inclined to fantasize. Talking with or reading the writings of people who know little or nothing about these matters is an unreliable way to try to acquire accurate information. Neither is it useful to participate in workshops or seminars which are persuasively promoted as opportunities to experience kundalini awakening or enlightenment.

In this kriya yoga tradition, extreme effort is never applied to awaken or work with kundalini energies. The most useful approach is to adopt lifestyle regimens and spiritual practices that can prepare the mind and body to be receptive, and to gently coax dormant forces to become active. They will then move and circulate as determined by the intelligence which is innate to them.

Clarity of awareness and feelings of lightness and exhilaration that may be experienced are normal. Uncontrolled laughing, crying, or other symptoms of emotional catharsis, should not be dramatized. Convulsive trembling, muscle twitching, or other erratic movements of the body should be avoided. If flows of energy seem to be too dynamic, inhale deeply, then exhale and relax. Encourage them to flow deeply within rather than allow physical or emotional reactions to occur.

Kundalini energies can be regulated by gentle application of will power or intention. Allow them to perform their transformative and awareness-clearing work. Avoid thinking that because you are aware of energy flows you should direct them to others in an endeavor to heal or help them. First help yourself to Self-realization. You will then be able to know how best to help others.

Visions, perceptions of brilliant light, a sense of the oneness of life and of having transcended the boundaries of space and time, feelings of love and compassion for all living things, and extreme joy may be experienced when the upward flowing currents of kundalini energy stimulate certain brain centers. While such perceptions can be enjoyable and attractive, it should be remembered that what is perceived is not what you are, or the ultimate realization to have.

Within the channel in the spine through which kundalini energies ascend are three channels, starting at the base chakra and going to the higher brain. The two outer channels have gross and subtle astral characteristics. The innermost channel, "the pathway of God," has fine causal characteristics. Meditators who are intent on Self- and God-discovery are advised to become aware of kundalini energies moving upward through this channel. Perceptions of mental and astral phenomena can then be more easily avoided.

During preliminary stages of meditation, when kundalini energies enliven the chakras, their sounds and lights may be perceived. As life force ascends through the central channel in the spine, it may be perceived as a pleasurable sensation or as a mild electric current. It may ascend smoothly to the crown chakra or its flow may be blocked at one of the chakras. If a blockage is encountered, do not despair; it will eventually be removed. Use the meditation techniques explained in these lessons. Hatha yoga and pranayama practice can be helpful, as can chiropractic adjustments. Cultivate devotion.

Your soul peace and clarity of awareness need not be determined by the actions of kundalini energies. If you do not feel their movements or experience their effects, you can still contemplate the truth of your being and the reality of God.

OVERCOMING THE THREE MAJOR OBSTACLES TO LIBERATION OF CONSCIOUSNESS

Yogic literature describes three obstacles which may interfere with the smooth flow of kundalini energies and frustrate the soul's urge to be fully awake. Described as "knots" or impediments which confine awareness, they are related to the base chakra, the fourth chakra, and the spiritual eye center:

1. <u>Obstacle related to the base chakra</u>. Strong attachment to the realm of nature, its objects and processes. This kind of attachment elicits desire for material things, sense pleasures, and to accomplish ego-driven goals. It keeps attention flowing outward, causes the mind to be restless, and interferes with meditative concentration.

This obstacle can be overcome by dispassionately relating to the realm of nature without mental or emotional attachment to it, and by regular practice of superconscious meditation.

2. <u>Obstacle related to the fourth chakra</u>. Attachment, which may be strong or weak, to sentimental feelings and thoughts, and to the urge to perform good deeds and be helpful to others.

This obstacle can be overcome by selflessly rendering useful service when possible, purifying the ego-sense, and aspiring to awaken to more refined levels of Self- and God-realization.

3. <u>Obstacle related to the spiritual eye chakra</u>. Attachment, which may be obvious or subtle, to subjective perceptions (visions, ecstasy, pleasant moods) and exceptional abilities and powers of perception which may accompany preliminary stages of Self-realization.

This obstacle can be overcome by withdrawing attention from and transcending mental and astral phenomena and contemplating the field of pure existence-being which is devoid of attributes.

> By the practice of yoga, restricting influences are weakened
> and clarification of awareness to the stage of discriminative
> discernment (enlightenment) is accomplished.
> – *Patanjali's yoga-sutras 2:28*

LESSON SIX / PART TWO

LIFESTYLE GUIDELINES

UNFOLD AND EXPRESS YOUR INNATE ABILITIES

> Focus your attention within. You will experience new power, new strength, and peace in body, mind and spirit. All bonds that limited you will be vanquished. – *Paramahansa Yogananda*

Because our behaviors and circumstances always correspond to our mental states and states of awareness, it is fairly easy to determine the degree and quality of our spiritual growth.

Habitual dramatization of dysfunctional behaviors and personal circumstances which are disordered or distressing, indicate that our awareness is clouded and fragmented and our knowledge of the facts of life is minimal or superficial. Skillful, appropriate performance of actions and well-ordered, supportive personal circumstances indicate healthy states of mind and awareness along with knowledge of how to live effectively and the willingness to do it.

Seven levels of soul awareness, each related to one of the chakras in the spine or brain, represent the progressive stages through which souls awaken from partial awareness to spiritual enlightenment and liberation of consciousness. Until awareness is established in Self- and God-realization, various characteristics related to each level may be present: a person whose knowledge of spiritual matters is minimal and who is addicted to sense-pleasures and material things may be compassionate and idealistic; a "saint" may have debilitating urges and habits to overcome. The fast way to experience authentic spiritual growth is to renounce and rise above states of awareness, mental states, relationships, and behaviors which are restrictive while cultivating conditions and behaviors which are supportive of your aspiration to be fully awake. Right personal endeavors and the actions of grace will enable you to prevail.

THE SEVEN LEVELS OF SOUL AWARENESS
AND THEIR COMMON CHARACTERISTICS

1. <u>Semiconsciousness</u>, a partially aware, blurred state, related to the first chakra at the base of the spine. Characteristics are mental and emotional dullness, apathy, boredom, and complacency. The physical body is believed to be the real being. Awareness is clouded. If one is religious, belief in God is considered to be more important than knowledge of God. Prayers may be directed to a concept or traditional idea of God. Activities may be survival-oriented or impelled by desires and whims. Intellectual powers are weak. Memories, habits, and acquired

behaviors determine one's states of awareness, mental attitude, and actions. Provincialism, narrow-mindedness, may be considered normal.

2. Dysfunctional self-consciousness, related to the second chakra at the sacrum region of the spine. Some common characteristics are mental confusion and conflicted emotional states. Egoism, the illusional sense of selfhood, is strong. Delusions (erroneous ideas) and illusions (misperceptions of observed circumstances) blur mind and awareness. Attachments, dependency, addictions, and self-defeating behaviors may be dramatized. Sensuality and personal relationships of all kinds may be considered to be of importance. Actions are often irrational and unpredictable. Neurotic needs, complaining, blaming others or circumstances for misfortune, irresponsibility, and fantasies may be habitual. Subconscious conditionings are strongly influential. A person who is religious may be inclined to become fascinated with past lives, mediumship (channeling), hypnosis, magic, angels, or mental or psychic phenomena. If meditation is practiced, one may be inclined to be preoccupied with subjective perceptions and pleasant moods.

3. Functional self-consciousness, related to the third chakra at the lumbar region of the spine. Usually a healthy-minded, but still ego-directed state of awareness. Thoughts may be rational and actions may be performed skillfully. Power, control, recognition, and accomplishment that will be long-remembered may considered to be of importance. Partial intellectual comprehension of one's true nature and the reality of God may be present, yet considered to be of less importance than activities that serve one's personal goals. Interest in spiritual matters may be related to a desire for self-improvement and improved personal circumstances. Spiritual growth may be thwarted by desire to perpetuate one's present status, to be more spiritually awake and functional without having to renounce egotism: the mistaken notion of being special or unique because of personal accomplishments. If meditation is regularly practiced to the stage of superconsciousness, the mind and awareness of the practitioner will be gradually purified.

4. Superconsciousness, related to the fourth chakra at the dorsal region of the spine. Self-realization may be experienced. Knowledge of being an individualized unit of one field of Consciousness prevails. When meditating, refined superconscious states and perceptions of God and of transcendent realities may be experienced. Ego is diminished and purified. Intellectual powers improve. Normal activities and relationships are harmonious. Love, hope, faith, and devotion to duties is considered to be of importance. Sentimental thoughts and feelings for the welfare of others which are mistaken for compassion may distract attention from spiritual practices.

The devotee may be inclined to be involved with well-intentioned but useless activities before emotional maturity and Self-realization have been actualized. Discipleship is easier. Addictive tendencies and other awareness-limiting characteristics and habits common to the first three levels fall away.

5. <u>Cosmic Consciousness</u>, related to the fifth chakra in the spine opposite the throat. At this level the universe is perceived as a manifestation of cosmic forces emanated from one field of Consciousness (God). Desire to acquire higher knowledge is compelling. The categories and processes of cosmic manifestations are intuitively comprehended. Exceptional abilities and powers of perception spontaneously unfold.

6. <u>God-Consciousness</u>, related to the sixth chakra, the spiritual eye center in the front region of the brain. God is partially or completely realized (apprehended and experienced). Any remaining troublesome subconscious conditionings are resisted, weakened, and neutralized by the superior influences of God-realization.

7. <u>Illumination of Consciousness</u>, related to the seventh chakra, in the upper region of the brain. The reality of God is apprehended and the actions of cosmic processes are understood. When one is absorbed in meditation, transcendent perceptions are common. When one is not meditating, enlightenment remains undiminished and behaviors are spontaneously appropriate. Delusions and illusions are absent.

For the devotee whose lifestyle is wholesome, whose aspiration to be enlightened is unwavering, and who meditates superconsciously, awakening through these stages of spiritual growth is progressive. Disordered living, doubts about one's capacity to make progress, and impatience interfere with spiritual growth. A tendency to be overly anxious in regard to spiritual growth should be renounced. If you know that you are doing your best, you have only to persist with firm resolve and faith. Satisfying results will be in accord with the duration of time that is required for psychological transformations to occur and for superconsciousness to be integrated with thoughts, emotions, mind, and body. Clarified awareness and a refined nervous system enable soul qualities and abilities to more easily emerge.

Awareness is clarified by rational thinking, emotional calmness, dispassionate behavior, and frequent superconscious meditation. The nervous system is refined by superconscious influences, flows of life force through the body (especially through the spine and brain when meditating, whether occurring spontaneously or caused to flow by practicing specific techniques), pure foods, fresh air, and sunlight.

If exceptional abilities and powers of perception are used only to fulfill mundane desires or to nurture egocentric inclinations, they can interfere with spiritual growth. While they may be used to fulfill life-enhancing desires and wholesome purposes, they should primarily be used to accomplish Self- and God-realization.

When your awareness is clarified before you are enlightened, life-enhancing desires and purposes can easily be fulfilled, supportive events and circumstances can be attracted, and all of your actions can be constructive. When necessary, and when appropriate to do so, you can cause constructive effects to occur by gentle intention or by simple faith rather than by extreme effort.

Although there is no need to desire to quickly unfold exceptional abilities or extraordinary powers of perception, don't be afraid to have them emerge. Your soul capacities will expand and your innate qualities will spontaneously blossom in accord with your receptivity.

Rather than try to develop powers of clairvoyance, levitate, or demonstrate minor miracles (the effects of little known natural laws), improve your understanding of your relationship to God and the universe, cultivate emotional maturity, and perform duties responsibly. There is no need to desire exceptional abilities if the skills you now have are not being effectively applied. When your life is well-ordered and your actions are purposeful, insights will be acquired, functional skills will improve, and satisfying spiritual growth will naturally occur. Your healthy states of mind and awareness and your useful actions will also benefit others and nurture the well-being of society.

Just as attempts to acquire exceptional abilities before one is emotionally mature and spiritually aware are futile, travels to teachers, ashrams, or other places of pilgrimage in a frantic quest for enlightenment will almost always result in disappointment.

THREE IMPORTANT THINGS TO KNOW

The three distinguishing characteristics of a God-focused life are:

1. Repentance. Errors of thinking, feeling, and behavior are readily acknowledged and better choices are made.

2. Commitment. Dedication to wholesome, constructive living and to one's spiritual path is resolute (firm, unwavering).

3. Participation. The practical means by which meaningful purposes may be accomplished and spiritual growth may be experienced are learned and skillfully performed.

Without repentance, debilitating modes of thinking, feeling and behavior may persist. Without commitment, confusion and indecision may prevail. Without intentional performance of constructive actions, little or nothing of value will be accomplished. Improvement, if any, will be the result of the remaining force of constructive thoughts or actions implemented in the past or the supportive influences of grace.

A devotee should not expect God, or others, to do what can and should be done for oneself. It should be understood that every rational person can learn to participate with the Power that enlivens the universe and energizes the processes of evolution. Personal circumstances are improved and spiritual growth is accelerated when thoughts and actions are in accord with the innate inclination of life to prevail.

THE TWO PRIMAL URGES THAT INFLUENCE OUR LIVES

Until spiritual enlightenment is flawless and permanent, the urge toward life (expansion of awareness, functional freedom, and Self- and God-realization) and the urge toward death (cessation of life) are compelling. The urge to live is the innate impulse of the soul. The urge to die is nurtured by a sense of helplessness and futility. (I have sometimes wondered: How many people who felt defeated by circumstances or were told that their illness was incurable, had they been informed of their possibilities and encouraged to live would have chosen not to depart from this world when they did?)

When the life-urge is strong, we willingly do everything we can to thrive and flourish. When the death-urge is allowed to be influential, we may be inclined to consciously or unconsciously cooperate in hastening the body's journey to the crematorium or grave by our negative thoughts and unwholesome behaviors. When both urges are influential, mental confusion, emotional conflict, and erratic lifestyle behaviors may be dramatized.

A truth student should understand that it is impossible for a soul to die (cease to exist). It can only be more, or less, awake as determined by its choices. What many people refer to as death is the demise of the physical body, not of the soul. Transition from the body, which eventually occurs for all incarnated souls, is but a minor episode among many which are experienced during the soul's sojourn in space and time. If, during or after transition the soul is not alert, after a period of rest and recovery it will begin to wake up. If it is semiconscious, it may experience dreams and visions as determined by the contents of the mind. Perceptions may be "heaven-like" or otherwise. If an urge to identify with a physical body is compelling, the soul may reincarnate to again experience mundane life in accord with its desires or inclinations. Or it may realize that reincarnation is unnecessary, that personal expression and spiritual growth can continue in subtle astral realms.

Affirm With Inspired Conviction
I joyously welcome the opportunities I have to creatively and constructively express my innate soul qualities and abilities.

MEDITATION

ROUTINES FOR ALL LEVELS OF PRACTICE

By practice of pranayama when feelings of attachment and aversion are banished, exceptional soul powers unfold. When restlessness ceases and life forces are harmonized, one's awareness can easily be absorbed in pure consciousness. Remaining thus established, one is liberated while embodied.

– Sri Yukteswar

Regardless of your degree of meditation skill, it is helpful to have a specific routine chosen for your purpose. Then when you sit, you will be able to immediately begin and to proceed for the duration of your practice session with alert attention.

Remember the usefulness of meditating at the same time every day (allowing for occasional disruptions in your schedule which may occur from time to time). Whatever is done on a regular schedule is anticipated. When meditation practice is anticipated, your thoughts will begin to settle down and desire to meditate will increase.

Avoid procrastination, making excuses, and laziness. Ask: What is my most important aim in life? You know the answer; it is to be Self- and God-realized. Knowing this, don't avoid doing the very thing that can be most helpful to you,

The tendency to allow thoughts, emotions, desires, awareness of duties and needs, and restlessness to determine your schedule of meditation practice should be resisted and overcome. Even when you do not feel inspired, meditate as a spiritual duty. If you do not feel that you can wholeheartedly pray or practice meditation techniques, at least assume a meditation posture and sit in the silence for a while to contemplate your relationship with the Infinite.

Avoid mental perversity: don't resist doing what you know to be for your highest good in a vain endeavor to assert or to maintain an emotionally immature sense of self-determinism or because you think you know what is best when you really do not.

Success in all worthwhile endeavors is more quickly accomplished by doing what needs to be done while avoiding what is nonessential or ineffective. The simple act of choosing to meditate on a regular schedule contributes to psychological transformation, because firm decisions resist and gradually overcome conditioned tendencies and habits which were formerly allowed to be influential.

The occasions of mild confusion in regard to one's life purpose which meditators may experience from time to time, are often due to the tension between the tendency to allow attention and energies to constantly flow outward and the inclination (and act) of consciously directing attention and energies inward when meditating. Inner conflict may also be experienced during the course of ordinary living because the exercise of choice and will to think and behave constructively may be opposed by habits or subconscious conditionings.

Any clean, quiet place is suitable for meditation practice. If you have a special place for this purpose, go there at the appointed time.

Having learned the meditation techniques described in the previous lessons, the question that may arise is: In what sequence should they be used?

ROUTINE FOR NEW MEDITATORS

Remind yourself that the primary purpose of meditation practice is to relax, calm the mind and emotions, and clarify awareness. Superconscious awareness cannot be experienced when the body is tense, the mind is flooded with thoughts and memories, emotions are unstable, or awareness is blurred. It can be helpful to remember the essence of the second verse of the first chapter of Patanjali's yoga-sutras: *Oneness is realized when the fluctuations (movements) in the meditator's field of awareness cease.* Be intent on having that experience.

Assume your meditation posture. Close your eyes. Withdraw your attention from externals and from the senses. Bring your attention (and feeling) up through the spine and into the brain. Look into or be aware at the spiritual eye center. Pray or invoke the Presence of God. If you pray, do so with soul-felt devotion, using simple words. To elicit awareness of the Presence of God:

• Open your mind and heart (being) to the Infinite.
• Acknowledge the saints and sages of all enlightenment traditions with a feeling of gratitude. If you are an initiated disciple of an enlightenment tradition, reverently acknowledge your teacher and the lineage of teachers.
• Acknowledge the innate, divine nature of all souls.
• Acknowledge the essence of your being; that you are established in the field of Infinite Consciousness and all knowledge of it and its processes is within you.

Use your mantra until your awareness is clear and tranquil, then rest at that stage for a while. Twenty to twenty-five minutes should be sufficient for one practice session.

If you want to continue beyond that stage, after resting for a while in the tranquil state, gently contemplate your relationship to the Infinite. Remain alert and attentive. Let your innate urge to have your awareness restored to wholeness determine your experience.

To conclude, open your eyes. Sit poised and relaxed for a few moments. Resume your normal activities. Optional: While resting in the calm state immediately following meditation practice, if you have a problem to solve, a decision to make, a need for healing, a desire to be fulfilled, or someone for whom to pray, address these matters while your mind is rational and your awareness is clear. Do not take these matters into meditation. Meditate only for the purpose of being soul- and God-conscious. Deal with mundane matters during the calm interlude after meditation practice.

This easy, beneficial meditation routine can be practiced once or twice a day by almost anyone. Proficiency in this procedure should be acquired before advanced techniques are learned or practiced.

ROUTINES FOR INTERMEDIATE PRACTICE

After you are proficient in using the basic routine, proceed to the intermediate stage, allowing thirty minutes or more for practice.

• Sit, pray and/or invoke the Presence of God.
• Use your mantra until you are calm and concentrated. Rest at that stage for several minutes, alert and attentive.
• If inner sounds are spontaneously heard, listen to them as taught in lesson two (technique of primordial sound contemplation). If sounds do not spontaneously emerge, listen until you hear them.
• After listening to inner sounds for a while, if you want to continue to meditate, use the technique to expand your awareness taught in lesson three.
• Conclude the practice session in the usual way.

ROUTINES FOR ADVANCED PRACTICE

After you are proficient in using the intermediate routine, proceed to advanced practice, allowing forty minutes to an hour per session.

• Start in the usual way.
• Listen to your mantra until your attention is internalized, then listen to Om.
• After Om contemplation, practice the technique taught in the fourth lesson to move your awareness through the chakras.
• After resting in the silence for a while, practice the "path of God" technique taught in lesson five. Feel the current of life force moving in the spine and brain.
• After using the "path of God" technique, sit in the silence listening to Om, then conclude the practice session in the usual way.

When you can practice these techniques easily, you may use them in the sequence that best suits your purpose without being confined to a specific routine. For instance: you may want to start with "path of God" breathing, then listen to Om. Just doing that may be sufficient. Use the other techniques to supplement your practice according to your inclination, especially when you notice that you are not alert because you are too passive. Techniques are "tools" to be used to accomplish a purpose. The results of practice are more important than the procedures which help to produce them.

Experiment until you discover the best meditation routine for you, and adhere to it. If, after a few months, your usual routine does not seem to be effective, or you are performing it mechanically, either apply yourself to it with more concentration or vary the routine so that your meditation practice will be interesting and productive.

Kriya yoga initiates should practice the meditation routines they learned at the time of initiation.

When sitting in the silence after practicing a technique, be sure to maintain an upright posture and an alert, attentive attitude. Keep your awareness in the spiritual eye and higher brain. Sitting like this, patiently waiting and watching, keeps the currents of life force flowing upward. In time, meditation will flow spontaneously. Always continue to meditate until subconscious resistance to practice ceases, the mind is calm, and superconsciousness is experienced.

OTHER USEFUL THINGS TO DO TO SUPPORT YOUR SPIRITUAL PRACTICES AND STABILIZE YOUR LIFE

Regular superconscious meditation will anchor you in the Infinite. To support your spiritual practices:

• After meditation, maintain your calm soul- and God-aware state. Superconsciousness will then pervade your mind and awareness at all times, even during the hours of sleep. (If you awaken at night, lie still, in a meditative state until you go back to sleep.) Do your best to live a balanced, wholesome, constructive, purposeful life.
• Avoid superficial or nonuseful talking with others about metaphysical ideas. Conserve your vital forces. Use them to further your spiritual growth and accomplish your purposes.
• Every day, read a few verses from your favorite scripture. The two basic texts for all kriya yoga practitioners to study are the Bhagavad Gita and the yoga-sutras.
• During the first year of intensive spiritual practice, study only the philosophical principles and adhere to the lifestyle regimens and meditation practices of this kriya yoga tradition. You will avoid mental confusion and be able to concentrate on applying yourself to practices essential to your well-being and spiritual growth.

Every one who hears these teachings and applies them can be compared to a wise person who built his house on a rock. The rain descended, the floods came, the winds blew, and beat upon that house; and it fell not: for was founded on a rock. – *Matthew 8:24,25 (Modern translation)*

REVIEW OF LESSON SIX

1. Where does the soul's life force enter the body?

    _____

2. What is the energy of kundalini?

    _____

3. What encourages kundalini forces to awaken?

    _____

4. How can the energy of kundalini be transferred from one person to another?

    _____

5. What is the cause of subjective perceptions (light, sound, pleasurable sensations, and other phenomena)?

    _____

6. Why should such perceptions be transcended?

    _____

7. What are the three major obstacles to spiritual growth to overcome? Why?

    1 _____ 2 _____

    3 _____   _____

8. List the seven levels of soul awareness.

    1 _____ 2 _____

    3 _____ 4 _____

    5 _____ 6 _____

    7 _____

PERSONAL APPLICATION

1. At what level of soul awareness do you ordinarily function? _____

2. What will you do to awaken to higher levels?

   _____

   _____

3. To make rapid progress on the spiritual path, what are three important things to do?

   1 _____

   2 _____

   3 _____

4. What are the two primal urges that influence our lives?

   1 _____   2 _____

6. When meditating, when your breathing becomes slow and refined, notice that thoughts and emotions are calm and more refined. During the brief pause after inhalation and exhalation, notice that your mind is devoid of thoughts. By becoming familiar with that state, you will be able to elicit it at will. You will soon be able to control your states of awareness by choice. When you sit to meditate, you will be able to quickly elicit a calm, superconscious state.

5. Review your meditation routine. Modify and improve it according to your need. When a routine is satisfying, continue with it.

7. After meditation practice, or anytime when you are alone and quiet, inquire into what you are at the innermost level of your being. You are not the mind which is subject to being modified. You are not your changeable moods. You are not your personality, the "mask" you wear to present yourself to others. You are not your body which was born and will cease to exist. Although your mind, emotional states, personality characteristics, and physical body have changed through the years, you have not changed. What is the essence of your being which observes, perceives, determines, and experiences, yet does not change? Discover it. Let your awareness always be anchored in it.

THE WISDOM OF THE AGES

Lead me from the unreal to the Real. Lead me from darkness to light. Lead me from death to immortality. – *Brihadaranyaka Upanishad (800 – 500 B.C.E.)*

At fifteen my mind was bent on learning; at thirty, I stood firm; at forty, I was free from delusions; at fifty, I understood the will of God; at sixty, my ears were receptive to the truth; at seventy, I could follow the promptings of my heart without overstepping the boundaries of [what is] right. – *Confucius (551 – 479 B.C.E.)*

Manifest plainness. Embrace simplicity. Reduce selfishness. Have few desires.
— The Way of Lao-tzu (600 B.C.E.)

This is the noble truth of the way which leads to the stopping of sorrow. [It is] the noble eightfold path: right views, right aspirations, right speech, right conduct, right livelihood, right endeavor, right mindfulness [alert awareness], and right contemplation.
— The Pali Canon, sayings attributed to the Buddha (500 B.C.E.)

The soul, when it shall have driven away from itself all that is contrary to the Divine Will, becomes transformed in God. – *Saint John of the Cross (1542 – 1591)*

There is not in the world a kind of life more sweet and delightful than that of a continual walk with God. Those only can comprehend it who practice and experience it.
– Brother Lawrence / The Practice of the Presence of God (1605 – 1691)

You can only apprehend the Infinite by a faculty superior to reason, by entering into a state in which you are a finite self no longer—in which the divine essence is communicated to you. This is ecstasy. It is the liberation of your mind from its finite consciousness. Like only can apprehend like; when you thus cease to be finite, you become one with the Infinite.
– Plotinus (205 – 270)

The Masters say that the soul has two faces [inclinations]. The higher one always sees God, the lower one looks downward and informs the senses. The higher one is the summit of the soul; it gazes into eternity. – *Meister Eckhart (1260 – 1327)*

Perform all your duties with your hands; let your heart be with God. – *Kabir (1440 – 1518)*

Settle yourself in solitude and you will experience God in yourself.
– Saint Teresa / The Interior Castle (1515 – 1582)

Egoism arises only in the absence of investigation of truth; when one enquires into the idea of ego, it ceases to exist and there is pure, infinite consciousness. Desireless, free from delusion, remain established in Self-knowledge.   *– Yoga Vasistha (circa 900 – 1300)*

LESSON SEVEN

PHILOSOPHY

SPIRITUAL ENLIGHTENMENT
AND SOUL LIBERATION

> In the highest state of consciousness you can maintain your divine realization while working, speaking, or moving about in this world. When it is permanent, there is no possibility of falling back into a state of delusion. – *Paramahansa Yogananda*

For many centuries, millions of sincere truth seekers have earnestly endeavored to become enlightened—and have failed to accomplish the desire of their heart (soul). They either did not know how to be receptive to spiritual growth or perhaps did not know that spiritual enlightenment is the result of awakening to conscious awareness of one's true nature rather than a state to be attained.

Spiritual enlightenment is real when we are fully aware of our true nature as an individualized aspect of one field of Consciousness (God) and flawless knowledge of the facts of life enables us to think rationally and live effectively.

• Spiritual enlightenment clarifies soul awareness.
• The light of the soul then illumines the mind.
• Self-realization enables us to discern that we are other than the mind or its actions.
• Subconscious conditionings (karmic influences) which were once compelling, are eliminated or transcended.
• Delusions are absent. Illusions cease.
• The error of presuming the Self to be other than an individualized aspect of the self-existing field of Consciousness ceases.
• Cosmic consciousness, intuitive apprehension of the wholeness of life, its characteristics and interactions, prevails.
• The physical body is vitalized by the superior influences of super-consciousness. The nervous system is enlivened. The brain is refined. Soul forces flow freely.
• Innate soul qualities and exceptional abilities spontaneously unfold. We no longer have to endeavor to express the qualities of faith, kindness, compassion, patience, generosity, and trust in God. Unconfined soul abilities enable us to concentrate, perceive the truth of what is observed, easily accomplish our purposes, and live without limitations of any kind.
• Living is enjoyable, creative, and freely expressive.
• When spiritual enlightenment is unwavering, when awareness is not clouded or fragmented and our attention is not distracted from the

Self- and God-realized state, we are permanently liberated from mental and physical conditions which once obscured our perception of the facts of life.

Spiritual enlightenment can be realized by right personal endeavor and the redemptive actions of grace. Right endeavor, may include:

• Mastery of mental attitude, thoughts, emotional states, impulses, desires, and behaviors to facilitate psychological transformation.
• Unwavering aspiration to be enlightened.
• Skillful performance of constructive actions that confirm the sincerity of one's aspiration to be fully enlightened.
• Adherence to wholesome lifestyle regimens.
• Superconscious meditation practice and meditative contemplation to apprehend the reality of God.
• Skillful practice of meditation techniques to enliven the nervous system and encourage the awakening of dormant soul forces.
• Intellectual and intuitive analysis of the nature of the soul, the categories of cosmic manifestation, and the reality of God.

Life-enhancing impulses that originate in the field of omnipresent Consciousness and in the essence of the soul are actions of grace because they are freely expressive. The actions of grace are always constructive, supportive, enlivening and redemptive, and prevail wherever there is receptivity to them. When we do not know how (or cannot) solve a personal problem, accomplish a worthwhile purpose, or improve our circumstances or relationships—and sudden insight, our unplanned right actions, or unexpected good fortune resolves these issues—grace did what we could not do. When meditation practice does not produce results and a spontaneous change of viewpoint occurs that enables us to experience a transcendent state or clearly apprehend knowledge of ourselves and God, grace is influential.

Successful endeavors to acquire accurate knowledge, master thoughts, feelings, and behaviors, and to meditate skillfully purify the intellect and clarify awareness. The final awakening to spiritual enlightenment is due to the actions of grace—which are influential when the soul's innate urge to have its awareness restored to wholeness is no longer resisted by the psychological and physical conditions which formerly existed.

If you are spiritually enlightened, you know that your clear state of awareness is your natural state which has always been what it is. Remain steadfast in the knowledge you have so that it will never again become obscured or "forgotten" because of mental confusion, apathy or disinterest, and your liberation will be assured.

If you are not yet enlightened, what are your thoughts and feelings when you contemplate the possibility?

• Have you resolutely decided to be spiritually enlightened? If you have, persist in your commitment. If not, decide now.

• Is your spiritual enlightenment of primary importance to you?

• Do you ardently yearn to be fully, spiritually awake?

• Do you believe that you can awaken to Self- and God-realization in this incarnation?

• Are you willing to learn how to remove mental, emotional, or physical obstacles to spiritual growth—and do it?

Many people who proclaim themselves to be sincere devotees on the spiritual path are primarily interested in reinforcing egocentric behaviors and improving their physical circumstances and personal relationships. They do not know that spiritual enlightenment assures complete fulfillment in all aspects of life.

When all restrictions are removed from the mind and intellectual and intuitive powers are fully developed, the self-luminous essence of our being is fully revealed.

> Liberation is that state in which realization of pure being is permanent. It is absolute when [only] one Consciousness is perceived to exist and its processes are perceived as its self-referring actions. Consciousness with attributes [God] has the characteristics of awareness, existence, and bliss. Absolute Consciousness is devoid of attributes.
> – *Patanjali's yoga-sutras 4:36-37*

Affirm With Soul-Aware Conviction
I choose to be spiritually enlightened and I always consistently demonstrate my resolve by wise, decisive actions.

Devotees who direct their attention to the Absolute, whose awareness
is absorbed in that, whose intent is to realize that, whose limitations
have been removed by knowledge, awaken to full liberation from which
there is no return [to former conditions].
– *Bhagavad Gita 5:17*

LIFESTYLE GUIDELINES

LET YOUR LIGHT SHINE

The four stages of spiritual progress are introspection, devotion, renunciation, illumination. Introspection is perception of the soul's qualities. Devotion is unconditional love for God. Renunciation is freedom from dominance of the ego. Illumination is realization of absolute oneness in God.

– *Lahiri Mahasaya*

How will you live when you are fully enlightened? How will you think and feel? What will you do? What kind of relationships will you have? What will be your circumstances?

There is no need to wait until you are fully enlightened; soul qualities can be expressed now. This moment, where you are, established in awareness of your true nature, selflessly perform constructive, appropriate actions which will enhance your life and benefit others and the environment. By doing this, your mind will be purified and illumined and you will have the full support of nature in everything that you do.

Three categories of karma (subconscious tendencies which may influence thoughts, choices, moods, and actions) are 1) tendencies which are being acquired now because of thoughts, feelings, desires, actions, and reactions; 2) compelling tendencies acquired in the past; 3) dormant tendencies which may be activated in the near or distant future.

Karma is the accumulated residue of mental impressions caused by past thoughts, feelings, reactions, and perceptions. It is only of the mind, not of the soul. Alert, soul-directed thinking and living prevents the accumulation of new karma. If it is known that compelling tendencies will have fortunate effects, they may be allowed to express and their force exhausted. If it is known that their effects will be unfortunate, they should be resisted and better choices implemented. Dormant tendencies can be disarmed and eliminated by constructive living and superconscious meditation practice. Life force circulated through the spine and brain during meditation, and flowing spontaneously at other times, also weakens and dissolves karmic patterns.

When subliminal influences have been weakened and neutralized, all that remains to be transcended are the influences of the three constituent attributes of nature: *sattva guna*, which contributes to order and harmony; *rajas guna*, which elicits passionate desires or cravings; *tamas guna*, which blurs awareness. Until rajasic and tamasic influences are transcended, it is best to cultivate the nurturing influences of sattva guna by doing what will nurture health and well-being and enhance spiritual awareness.

Until sattvic characteristics prevail, the characteristics of the other two attributes are usually present. Eventually, the influences of the attributes of nature which pervade the mind, body, and environment are to be transcended by the devotee of God who aspires to liberation of consciousness. Tamas causes the unenlightened soul to be attached to indolence and ignorance. Rajas causes attachment to sensory stimulation, restlessness, and emotion-driven behaviors. Sattva causes attachment to pleasure, including pleasurable meditative perceptions.

In the Bhagavad Gita, Arjuna (the truth-seeking soul) asks:

> What are the characteristics of one who has transcended the attributes of nature? How does that person behave? And how does one go beyond the attributes? – *14:21*

Krishna (enlightened awareness) reveals:

> Such a one neither hates nor desires the presence or absence of the influences of the attributes of nature. That one who is unconcerned [because soul-centered and peaceful] and is not disturbed by the attributes of nature; who does not waver [in that knowledge]; to whom discomfort and pleasure are the same; who abides in the Self; to whom praise, blame, honor, and dishonor are the same; who is dispassionate in regard to friends and foes and has renounced all self-serving tendencies, is said to have transcended [the influences of] the attributes of nature. *– 14:22 – 25*

An enlightened person, not influenced by subliminal tendencies and ever aware of the difference between the essence of being and the actions of the mind, body, and nature, is not blindly involved with thoughts, emotions, relationships, or circumstances. Life can then be lived wisely, creatively, and spontaneously.

Thoughts and actions are wise when they are appropriate or ideal for the situation or purpose. Creativity nurtures new, innovative and useful ideas and behaviors. Functional freedom is possible because an enlightened person's awareness is neither conflicted by erroneous opinions nor fragmented by illusions. Spontaneousness—which should not be confused with impulsiveness or erratic, irrational behavior—is natural to the soul when restrictive psychological conditions have been eradicated or transcended.

When the devotee perceives the uselessness of ordinary, self-conscious life, but has not yet awakened to the stage at which the illusional sense of selfhood is purified and a clear sense of meaningful purpose is known, the major challenge may be that of knowing what to do. What was formerly of interest is no longer appealing. Desires diminish in intensity. Personal needs are few. Aspiration to be fully, spiritually awake may waver. One may be inclined to live aimlessly, be apathetic and lazy, ponder the possibility of reverting to former behaviors and circumstances in order to have a degree of comfort or enjoyment, or look for a new or different approach to spiritual growth. One may endeavor to escape into fantasy by mistakenly thinking that enlightenment has been accomplished, or become frantic in a desperate quest for higher understanding.

What is most needed at this time is a balance of aspiration, faith and patience, a well-ordered lifestyle, gentle persistence in spiritual practice, and selfless service performed in accord with abilities and resources. Avoid extreme effort in endeavors to accomplish purposes or to force spiritual growth. Learn to accomplish worthwhile purposes by being in the flow of resources and supportive events and relationships. Facilitate progressive spiritual growth by removing mental and physical obstacles to its emergence.

When performing selfless service and when engaged in meditation or other spiritual practices, do what you know to be effective and let the results be what they will be. You will then not be anxious about the outcome of what you do. You will not be elated when results are exceptional or unhappy when they are not. When endeavoring to help others, avoid thoughts and feelings of failure or rejection when your best efforts seem to be inadequate or when they are not appreciated. Nurture the understanding that the good you appear to do is really flowing through you, not from you. By being a conduit through which others and the environment are benefited, though your motives and actions are selfless, you also benefit.

When praying for others or providing assistance, avoid thinking that you are accumulating good karma or that God will bless you for your good works. Banish the idea of duality, the mistaken notion that God is apart from you. God is individualized as you. Because the omnipresent field of God is the only reality, you abide in the Presence of God which is through you and around you.

When you meditate correctly, you are not endeavoring to establish a connection with God; you are removing from your mind and awareness the conditions which restrict your perception of what you are and what God is. When you serve others in appropriate ways and nourish the environment, you are selflessly participating with the processes of evolution which nurture and support all aspects of life.

For where your treasure is, there will your heart be also.
– *New Testament* / *Matthew 6:21*

THE DEDICATED LIFE

INITIATION AND COMMITMENT TO DISCIPLESHIP

> One whose innate knowledge and exceptional abilities are fully awakened comprehends the wholeness of God and all souls as units of God's consciousness. Thus comprehending, one completely abandons the illusion of existence separate from God. This unification of awareness with God is the ultimate aim [of every unenlightened soul]. – *Sri Yukteswar*

Commitment to discipleship (continued learning, constructive living, and right spiritual practice) is essential for every person who yearns to be fully awake in God.

Paramahansa Yogananda once said, "The possibilities for having new perceptions and experiences are endless."

A disciple asked, "Will such possibilities never have an end?"

Paramahansaji replied, "Yes, when you experience endlessness [the absolute realization which permanently removes awareness from names and forms]."

To a disciple who asked how he might know when he was Self-realized, Paramahansaji said, "You will know, when you know."

Until enlightenment (clarified awareness along with knowledge of the reality, categories, and processes of Consciousness) is permanent, discipleship is necessary.

The two major obstacles to learning and spiritual growth which must be renounced are flagrant egotism and a perverse mental attitude, both of which incline one to resist new, useful ideas and refuse to conform to ideal modes of thinking and behavior. If you are aware of tendencies to be egotistical or mentally perverse, pray for strength of character and cultivate humility. If you lack knowledge of how to live effectively and of higher realities, admit it to yourself, and acquire knowledge. If you are not yet living the way you know you should (and really want to), learn how, and do it.

This path is not for one who is neurotic or lazy; it is for the sincere, healthy-minded, intentional devotee who ardently aspires to be fully awake and who is one hundred percent dedicated to right living and spiritual growth. It is then easier to make right choices and to discard debilitating mental attitudes, moods, beliefs, habits, behaviors, and relationships. Confusion, doubt, emotional instability, addictive behaviors, immorality, dishonesty, deviousness, egotism, pride, prejudice of any kind, provincialism, arrogance, emotional immaturity, selfishness, abject ignorance, apathy, and preference for fantasy rather than for valid knowledge, make it difficult if not impossible to be successful on the discipleship path.

INITIATION, AND ADVANCED MEDITATION PRACTICES

In this kriya yoga tradition, an opportunity to be initiated is made available when the devotee is sufficiently prepared. Before initiation, one should have at least a partial understanding of what God is; the true nature of the soul; the impersonal laws which determine the processes of causes and effects; how souls awaken through the stages of spiritual growth; and how to facilitate spiritual growth. The applicant should be living a wholesome life, be a regular meditator, and be sincere. Further, one should have respect for the tradition and the teacher of that tradition; be willing to learn and to practice what is learned; and have the intellectual capacity to learn and the functional capacity to apply what is learned.

Because the transmission of spiritual force is an essential aspect of initiation, before initiating a new disciple the teacher meditates to attune his or her awareness to the Infinite and the lineage of teachers of this kriya yoga tradition. Lifestyle regimens are then reviewed and special meditation techniques are taught, which are easy to learn if one has been skillfully practicing the preliminary techniques and routines described in lessons one through six.

Three techniques are taught at the first initiation: a procedure used to awaken dormant energies in the lower chakras; a pranayama used to direct flows of life force through the spine and brain; a technique used to contemplate inner light and sound.

The new initiate is instructed to practice the pranayama routine fourteen times once or twice a day for several months. Permission may then be given to increase the number. When done correctly, this technique enables the meditator to feel flows of life force in the spine. Kriya yoga gurus teach that this process quickens the devotee's spiritual evolution because of the greatly improved powers of meditative concentration that result and the rapid psychological and physical transformations that may occur. It magnetizes the spine, calms the mind, weakens harmful subliminal tendencies, clarifies the meditator's awareness, unstresses and refines the nervous system, and creates new nerve pathways in the brain.

After one or two years of regular practice of kriya pranayama and the supplemental techniques, more meditation methods may be learned. It is not useful to think that the advanced techniques must be learned quickly. The basic procedures which are taught when one is first initiated are more than adequate to enable one to become proficient in eliciting refined states of superconsciousness.

Although the pranayama technique that the new initiate learns is often referred to as kriya yoga practice, which it is, it is only one aspect of the complete system which includes right living regimens, practices to effect psychological transformation, study of higher realities, and surrendering the illusional sense of selfhood in favor of awakening to Self-realization. Many devotees who practice these meditation methods fail to experience spiritual growth because they erroneously think that right living, right thinking, and right behavior are not as important as meditation practice.

Even though kriya meditation techniques may be skillfully practiced, if one's lifestyle is not wholesome and constructive, if dysfunctional mental attitudes and behaviors have not been renounced, little or no progress will occur.

Teachers of this tradition say that daily circulation of life force through the vital centers in the spine and head produces beneficial changes in the brain that would otherwise require many years of natural evolution. Sunlight, fresh air, pure water, nutritious food, optimism and cheerfulness, mental calmness, emotional peace, good health, and environmental harmony allow the brain to be gradually refined. When these ideal conditions prevail, regular, right practice of kriya meditation techniques greatly accelerate the process.

Initiation is transformative and of real value when the applicant is fully prepared, commitment to discipleship is total, and instruction and spiritual energies are transmitted by a representative of this kriya yoga tradition who is qualified to do it. To be qualified to initiate, one must be a Self-realized initiate-practitioner of kriya yoga or an authorized representative of a Self-realized guru of this tradition. If these conditions do not prevail, instruction is only the sharing of information and is of little value.

A person who is not fully prepared, who is not willing to commit to discipleship, should not ask to be initiated. Nor should initiation be requested merely because one is curious or has a faint hope that it might be helpful. Initiation is a "new beginning," a transitional event that marks the moment in time when the devotee renounces ordinary ideas and habits, acquires higher knowledge, firmly resolves to live with conscious intention, and is empowered to do so.

LIGHT ON THE KRIYA YOGA PATH

While respect for one's teacher and the lineage of teachers is essential for a kriya yoga initiate, it is not recommended that they be worshipped. Paramahansaji said, "I am not the guru. God is the guru; I am God's servant." Inwardly aware of his relationship with God and willing to outwardly play the role of being a guru for the benefit of others, he always directed a disciple's attention and devotion to the Source.

Occasionally, a person who was initiated by a representative of Paramahansa Yogananda's organization or a former minister of the organization, informs me that Paramahansaji is their guru. An illusion which influences the thinking of many naive people is that they can have a meaningful relationship with a spiritual teacher whom they have never met, do not know, and who does not know them. It is unfortunate that many thousands of people indulge in this kind of fantasy.

Paramahansaji said, "After I am gone, some people will claim to be receiving messages from me or the other gurus. Do not believe them. Enlightened souls never speak through mediums."

Disembodied souls do not casually converse with egocentric people in the mundane realm. People who say that souls residing in subtle realms speak to or through them are delusional or dishonest, and should be avoided.

If disembodied saints are not easily accessible, what are we to think in regard to reports of positive response to prayers which are directed to them? Response to prayer is in accord with one's faith or from God. One's concept of a saint (or God) may be a point-of-contact with God. If the reality of God cannot be apprehended, prayer directed to a name or form envisioned as being an aspect of God may enable the petitioner's awareness to merge with the omnipresent field of Consciousness and be receptive to its supportive inclinations.

During my guru's lifetime, he privately ordained several disciples, authorized them to teach and initiate students, and said that some of them would have disciples. In 1951, he publicly announced that James J. Lynn (a spiritually advanced disciple to whom he had given the monastic name Rajasi Janakananda) would be his spiritual representative as president of the organization.

After Paramahansji's transition, Mr. Lynn told some of his brother and sister disciples, "Paramahansa Yogananda will always be our guru. There will never be another guru at the head of this organization." Although his humility and kind words reassured the disciples to whom he spoke, they did not accurately communicate the fact that, for the teachings and spiritual force of this kriya yoga tradition to continue to be enlivening and transformative, they must be transmitted through a lineage of empowered gurus.

When Paramahansa Yogananda ordained me, in 1951, he placed his hands on my head and said, "Teach as I have taught. Heal as I have healed. Initiate devotees of God into kriya yoga."

A young male disciple, who witnessed my ordination, asked, "Sir, is Roy to give initiations?" Our guru's response was immediate and explicit: "You, also, should do it. The same God that is in me, is in you. What I have done, you should do."

Since then, almost all of Paramahansaji's disciples have passed from this world. Of the few who remain, I am his only guru-successor. A few of his disciples teach the philosophical principles and practices of kriya yoga; I speak for, serve, and represent the tradition. It is my mission, which my guru confirmed.

Enlightened teachers never claim to be exclusive custodians of liberating knowledge or the source of influential power that redeems souls. This knowledge is for everyone who is receptive to it. God is the true guru (remover of delusions). Because knowledge of God is not easily acquired by people whose awareness is ordinary (blurred and fragmented), access to a spiritually awake teacher can be helpful. Even then, the teacher can only instruct; the student must do the necessary work, grow to emotional and spiritual maturity, and be receptive to the actions of grace.

I was initiated by my guru in the month of August, 1950, after eight months of preparation under his guidance. I had received his energy transmission a few weeks after our first meeting and had been meditating on a regular schedule. Following my initiation, he put his hands on my forehead and enabled me to see a brilliant light in the spiritual eye center.

Before I was initiated, I meditated for two or more hours daily, using the hong-sau mantra and listening to the Om vibration. After being initiated, I meditated four hours during the early morning from 3 a.m. to 7 a.m. and two or more hours each evening. My meditative perceptions were rarely exceptional. The most usual experiences were deep peace and vivid awareness of the essence of being in relationship to the wholeness of life. Occasionally, during interludes of "waiting and watching" after using a meditation technique, visions (which I understood to be mental phenomena) and fleeting episodes of expanded awareness would spontaneously occur.

When I was not meditating, I was aware of the psychological and physical changes that were occurring. My intellectual and intuitive powers of discernment improved, as did my understanding of the philosophical principles upon which the practice of yoga are based.

From time to time, when I visited my guru at his desert retreat house in Twentynine Palms or in Los Angeles, he would check my practice of meditation techniques and give personal advice. He never asked me about my meditation schedule or inner experiences. Now and then he would say, "You are making good progress; whatever you are doing, keep doing it."

Whenever we talked privately, Paramahansaji always spoke reverently about God and of the importance of being in tune with the gurus. He often told me, "Stay in tune with me. When you are in tune with me I can more easily help you. Lack of attunement causes static in the mental radio." Mental and spiritual attunement with the guru enables the disciple to be receptive to the telepathic and spiritual radiations which the guru emanates. I discovered that when I was attuned to Paramahansaji's mind and consciousness, I was aware of an inner strength, meditation practice was more effective, and my intuitive perceptions of higher realities were more vivid.

A guru's function is to assist the disciple to complete liberation of consciousness; as described in Patanjali's yoga-sutras (4:30–32):

> With the dawning of knowledge that accompanies Self- and God realization, all obstructions and restrictions cease to be influential. With their dissolution, the Self reclaims omnipresence. With the dawning of that knowledge, the cosmic forces, having served their purposes, also cease to be influential.

The personal obstructions that are eliminated are the delusions, illusions, subliminal tendencies, instinctual drives, and psychological conflicts which formerly blurred the soul's awareness. When these are no longer influential, the liberated soul's awareness is removed from the influences of the cosmic forces regulated by the three attributes of nature (gunas) which serve the purpose of producing and maintaining a universe, minds, and physical bodies. An enlightened person may still relate to the mundane realm and express through a mind and body while not being overly influenced by them.

A kriya initiate whose affiliation with a traditional religion is meaningful need not forsake it. Vocational, marital, social, cultural, and other secular circumstances are a matter of personal preference. Activities and relationships should be wholesome and constructive.

Kriya yoga teachers do not attempt to convert or persuade, nor do they accept money for personal spiritual instruction or initiation. Donations for charitable purposes may be accepted.

Initiates should maintain open communication with their teacher or the teacher's representative to ensure that they continue to have instruction and encouragement.

Shortly before his transition, Paramahansa Yogananda met with a few disciples to tell them how to serve truth seekers in the near and distant future. He said, "Many people, who come to us study for two or three years and we initiate them, think they have gotten from us all we have to offer. They go away to study something else or they lose interest in their practices. They then do not have the benefit of our support when they need it and we do not have the benefit of their company and their support for the work. For the past thirty years I have been very generous in making these teachings available. From now on, we must emphasize the unique value of initiation and the importance of sustained study and participation."

During more than four decades of teaching these principles and offering kriya yoga initiation in many countries of the world, I have also noticed that, of the many thousands of individuals whom I have instructed and initiated, only a few continue to practice. Many people who had good intentions when they began their participation either did not make a commitment to discipleship when they were initiated or they allowed their attention to be distracted.

The inclination to identify with conditioned states of mind and awareness and to allow ordinary self-conscious (egocentric) interests to determine one's life is influential until the urge to be spiritually awake prevails. This characteristic of the human condition was noted centuries ago by the author of the Bhagavad Gita (7:3):

> One among a thousand strives for perfection. Of those who strive, and of those who are [somewhat] accomplished, rarely does even one know the truth.

Many people are spiritually impoverished because they do not consider spiritual growth to be as important as their other purposes. Restless and confused, influenced by subconscious conditionings and the opinions and behaviors of others, they use their energy and skills primarily to fulfill desires, satisfy physical and emotional needs, or acquire social status. Seldom do they enjoy an interlude of silence or use even a small portion of their intellectual ability to discover their true nature and their relationship to the Infinite.

A disciple who is committed to spiritual growth awakens from sleep with thoughts of God and starts each day with meditation practice. Thus firmly established in God-awareness, life is lived with conscious intention. Thinking is rational. Choices are wise. Perceptions are accurate. Emotions are controlled. Time and energy are used efficiently. Actions are appropriate and productive.

It can also be helpful to annually renew your commitment to discipleship. On a calendar or in a private journal, mark the date and time when you were initiated. Each year, remember the occasion. Be thankful for the opportunity that was made available to you. Rededicate yourself to right living and spiritual practice. Examine your mental attitude, lifestyle, relationships, and major goals and purposes. Review the meditation techniques to be sure you are practicing correctly and effectively. Review your meditation routine; if necessary, improve it. Meditate longer than usual. Perform a charitable act.

HOW TO PREPARE FOR INITIATION

When you are familiar and comfortable with these teachings and practices, your initiation experience and affiliation with this enlightenment tradition will be more beneficial and meaningful.

• Study these lessons frequently.
• Adopt the recommended lifestyle guidelines.
• Practice the recommended meditation methods and routines on a regular schedule for six months to one year.
• When possible, participate in out retreats and programs.
• Prayerfully think about the responsibilities of discipleship. Be certain that you are making the right choice.

REVIEW OF LESSON SEVEN

1. What are some of the results of spiritual enlightenment?

   _____

   _____

   _____

2. What are some of the things you can do to be enlightened? Do them.

   _____

   _____

   _____

3. What are two major obstacles to learning and spiritual growth?

   1 _____ 2 _____

4. Are you clinging to any delusions (erroneous opinions). If so, renounce them.

5. Are you illusional (prone to make mistakes when perceiving ideas or circumstances)? If so, improve your powers of intellectual and intuitive discernment. Use common sense.

6 What are some of the requirements for kriya initiation?

   _____

   _____

   _____

7. If you are a kriya initiate, rededicate yourself to discipleship.

8. If you are not yet a kriya initiate, and would like to be initiated, prepare for it. Be sure it is a step you really want to take. When you are certain, be prepared to commit your life to right living and intentional spiritual practice—to be a disciple.

PERSONAL APPLICATION

Letting Your Light Shine

Sit quietly for a few moments. Be a possibility-thinker. Imagine the useful things you can do to benefit others and the planet. Don't wait until you are fully enlightened to let your light shine. If you are working at a job or are self-employed, don't wait until you retire to let your light shine.

1. What knowledge do you have which can be used to benefit others and the planet?

   _____

2. How can you most effectively apply your knowledge?

   _____

3. What skills and abilities do you have which can be used to benefit others and the planet?

   _____

4. How will you use your skills and abilities for these purposes?

   _____

5. What other resources do you have which can be used to benefit others and the planet?

   _____

6. How will you use your resources for these purposes?

   _____

   If you are unable, at this time, to perform helpful acts on behalf of others, acknowledge the innate, divine nature of all people and pray for their well-being and spiritual growth. Perhaps you can volunteer your services to an organized activity which is doing good work or support a ministry which spiritually educates and encourages truth-seekers. Remember, your participation must be selfless. Avoid being so emotionally involved that you become tired or confused. Maintain a daily schedule of meditation practice to refresh your mind and body and keep your awareness clear. Let thoughts, impulses, and actions be soul-directed.

HOW TO APPLY FOR INITIATION

When you are prepared, you may apply for initiation with this form. Please write clearly. Provide the information requested. Send a copy to our office.

Age _____ Married [ ] Single [ ] Occupation or Profession _____ Retired [ ]

How long have you been a member of Center for Spiritual Awareness? _____

Have you participated in our meditation retreats at Lakemont or elsewhere? yes [ ] no [ ]

Are you in good health? yes [ ] no [ ] If not, explain: _____

_____

What other religious, yoga, or metaphysical systems have you studied or practiced?

_____

_____

What books by Roy Eugene Davis have you read? _____

_____

Have you carefully studied the *Seven Lessons in Conscious Living*? yes [ ] no [ ]

Do you understand the philosophical principles described in these lessons? yes [ ] no [ ]

Is your lifestyle wholesome and constructive? yes [ ] no [ ]

Do you practice the meditation techniques on a regular schedule? yes [ ] no [ ]

How long have you been meditating? _____

Why do you want to be initiated? _____

Can you attend a retreat at CSA headquarters during the summer when initiation is offered? [ ] yes no [ ]. If not, perhaps you can attend one our seminars in another city. If you cannot attend a retreat or seminar, mark here [ ]. *Note:* Kriya initiates are welcome to attend our initiation services to review their practice and renew their commitment to discipleship.

This my application for initiation into kriya yoga and its practices. I understand that what I will learn is for my use only. I will not discuss the meditation techniques with others unless given permission to do so. _____   _____
                                               signature   month day year

Your Name _____

Address _____

_____

Country if outside the U.S. _____

CENTER FOR SPIRITUAL AWARENESS • P.O. BOX 7 • LAKEMONT, GEORGIA 30552 (U.S.A.)

Glossary

Some words are *italicized* when defined or for special emphasis. The eras B.C. and A.D. are designated as B.C.E. (before the current era) and C.E. (current era).

Absolute The transcendent field of pure Consciousness.

actualize To make real or bring into manifestation. Abilities are actualized when they are expressed or demonstrated. Goals are actualized when they are accomplished. Purposes are actualized when they are fulfilled.

advaita Nonduality, oneness. When the intellect is purified and intuition is unveiled, all of the categories and processes of Consciousness are clearly apprehended.

agni Fire. One of five primary element influences in nature. It causes psychological and bio-chemical transformations. An aspect of agni energizes the mind, manifests the radiance of health in the body, and influences eyesight. Agni is also evident as the divine force and illumined will that can manifest the soul's potential for growth and expression.

agnosticism The theory that, while not denying the existence of God, asserts that God cannot be known. An agnostic adheres to the opinion that only perceived phenomena are objects of exact knowledge. See *atheism* and *deism*.

ahamkara The illusional sense of "I-ness" (self-identity). When the soul does not discern the difference between itself as pure awareness and its illusional sense of selfhood, a mistaken presumption of independent existence results.

ashram A quiet, secluded abode for study and spiritual practice. An ashram provides a supportive environment where spiritual aspirants can live without distractions.

astral realm The realm composed of life forces. Souls come from this realm into physical incarnation and return to it between incarnations. Spiritually advanced souls may pass through it to continue their awakening in finer causal realms, or transcend involvement with all aspects of Primordial Nature. See *causal realm*.

atheism Disbelief in or denial of the existence of God. See *agnosticism* and *deism*.

atman Also *atma*. The true essence of every person and creature. The individualized field of awareness which, when identified with mind and matter is referred to as a soul. Spelled with an upper case "*A*" the word is used to refer to the Supreme Being. *Paramatman* (*para*, beyond) is the field of pure Consciousness.

avatar The emergence and manifestation of divine qualities and powers in human form. An enlightened soul that incarnates for the purpose of infusing planetary consciousness with divine influences. The "universal avatar" concept is that divine qualities are unveiled as individual and collective consciousness is illumined.

avidya Not-knowledge, in contrast to *vidya*: knowledge of God's reality and its aspects and categories of manifestation.

Ayurveda *Ayus*, life; *veda*, knowledge. A natural way to nurture total well-being that evolved in India thousands of years ago. According to tradition, it was taught to sages by the gods. Ayurvedic diagnostic procedures include examination of the patient's pulse, temperature, skin condition, eyes, psychological characteristics, behavior, and other factors. Treatment includes recommendations of foods and herbs for specific purposes, attitude adjustment, behavior modification, detoxification regimens, meditation practice, and other procedures used to restore balance to the patient's mind-body constitution.

Lifestyle regimens are prescribed to balance the three *doshas*, the subtle governing principles (*vata*, space-air; *pitta*, fire; *kapha*, water-earth) which determine physiological functions and influence psychological states. Foods are recommended according to how their tastes (sweet, sour, salty, pungent, bitter, astringent) influence the governing principles. Food transformation is said to progress through seven stages: plasma, blood, muscle, fat, bone, bone marrow and reproductive essences.

In the *Charaka Samhita*, a primary Ayurvedic text, over five hundred herbs are listed with descriptions of their medicinal uses. Knowledge of Ayurveda flowed from India to Tibet, China, and Mediterranean countries, and more recently to the West. During the years of British rule in India, although state patronage resulted in the decline of Ayurvedic practice in the urban centers, it continued to be the treatment of choice among rural populations. There are now several Ayurvedic colleges in India and in other countries and scientific research is underway to investigate and endeavor to validate these wellness procedures.

Siddha Medicine, a similar wellness system, evolved in the southern region of India. Its many texts are believed to have been written by enlightened saints, among whom Agastya is especially revered. Practitioners of Siddha Medicine regimens may also prescribe the use of the ashes of gems and purified metals for healing and rejuvenation purposes. Thousands of years ago, yogis researched, discovered and used various means of ensuring healthy, long life for the purpose of allowing them to accomplish soul liberation. Some of their knowledge was made available for the welfare of people in secular society.

Babaji Guru of Lahiri Mahasaya. *Baba*, father; *ji*, used at the end of a name to indicate respect. In Asia, many venerated male saints are referred to as Baba or Babaji. Mahavatar (*maha*, great; *avatar*, incarnation or manifestation of divine qualities). Babaji is the name used to refer to the enlightened saint who revived the ancient kriya yoga teachings and practices and made them more widely available in India during the nineteenth century.

Bhagavad Gita Holy or Divine Song. From *bhaj*, to revere or love; *gai*, song. A scripture treasured by millions of people in which Krishna (enlightened consciousness) is portrayed as a divine incarnation who teaches his disciple Arjuna "the eternal way of righteousness" and the ways of knowledge, selfless service, devotion, and meditation. Frequent reading of the Bhagavad Gita can purify the mind and awaken innate spiritual qualities.

Mahavatar Babaji

Bhagavan Lord, that which rules. One who is endowed with the six attributes of infinite spiritual power, righteousness, glory, splendor, knowledge, and renunciation.

bhakti Fervent love for God which can result in God-realization and perception of the innate divinity of every person and creature. Love purifies the mind and unveils the soul's qualities.

bliss The unadulterated joy of awareness of pure being, rather than mental happiness or an emotional mood.

Brahma The expanding, projecting aspect of the Godhead which emanates the universe. *Vishnu* is a name for the aspect of God which preserves and maintains the universe. *Shiva* is a name for God's transformative aspect which dissolves forms and circumstances to allow new expressions. Shiva is also considered to be Supreme Consciousness. *Shakti*, the cosmic creative energy of Supreme Consciousness, is referred to as its feminine expression that manifests and enlivens the worlds.

brahmacharya God-centered behavior or conduct. Regulation of vital forces and of mental, sensory, and emotional tendencies and behaviors for the purpose of conservation, wise use, and transmutation of energies, freeing them to be used for intentional living and dedicated spiritual practices. Transmuted energies increase reserves of refined energy that contribute to overall health and vitality.

Brahman The Supreme Reality, the Absolute.

Buddha A seer who lived in northern India about 500 B.C.E. Of royal birth, as a young man he became troubled when he learned of the sufferings of the average person in society. After marrying, and fathering a son, he left home to seek higher knowledge. Following a duration of ascetic yogic practice, he adopted "the middle way" of reasoned moderation and awakened to illumination of consciousness. He then walked through the Ganges Valley for almost half a century, teaching and forming a society of renunciates. He taught love, nonhatred, dedication to truth, the elimination of wishful thinking, and nondependence upon externals. In Buddhism, spiritual enlightenment is realization of the True Self which is common to all.

buddhi Verb-root *budh*, to know. Because all souls are expressions of one Consciousness, all have a "buddha nature." When it is directly experienced, *nirvana*, the "extinguishing" of the illusional sense of selfhood results.

capacity The capability to receive or contain. The ability to use skills and accomplish purposes. Right living and spiritual practices increase one's capacity to accomplish purposes and to more easily apprehend and experience the reality of God.

causal realm The realm of electric and magnetic properties preceding astral and physical manifestation. Souls residing here return to an astral incarnation or continue to awaken to transcendent realizations. See *astral realm.*

chakra A vital center in the body through which the soul's vital forces are distributed. Located in the spinal pathway, between the eyebrows, and the upper brain. *See lesson five for descriptions of the chakras.*

chitta The awareness of the individualized Self identified with the mind and its contents and transformations. The natural state of the Self is *samadhi* (wholeness).

chitti Pure Consciousness.

christ Latin *christus*, from Greek *khristos*, anointed, and *kriein*, to anoint (with oil, as a religious rite). In some Western philosophical systems the aspect of God that pervades the universe is referred to as Christ Consciousness because the manifest realms are considered to be anointed with God's presence. One who has realized the all-pervading reality of God may thus be said to be Christ-conscious.

consciousness In ordinary usage, the state of being aware. The metaphysical meaning is the reality of God, souls, and all aspects and forms of nature.

cosmic consciousness Awareness, which may be partial or complete, of Consciousness and its aspects as a continuum or wholeness. Cosmic consciousness usually unfolds gradually. It can be nurtured by renouncing egocentric attitudes and behaviors and by aspiration to spiritual growth, prayer, and meditation. When superconsciousness influences ordinary waking states, cosmic consciousness progressively unfolds. It can also emerge suddenly.

Cosmic Mind The one Mind of which individualized minds are aspects or parts. Mental states, subliminal tendencies, thoughts, desires, and intentions interact with Cosmic Mind which is inclined to manifest corresponding conditions and circumstances.

deism Belief that God created the universe, but is removed from it, has no influence on phenomena, and provides no supernatural revelation. See *agnosticism* and *atheism*.

delusion An erroneous or invalid belief or opinion. The initial intellectual error from which all other delusions and their consequences result is presuming the true Self to be mind or matter. See *ego*, *illusion*, and *tapasya*.

deva That which shines, a god. In some philosophical systems the gods (*devas*) and goddesses (*devis*) are considered to be spiritually radiant souls dwelling in subtle or celestial realms. The gods are more accurately defined as cosmic forces which regulate universal processes and can be invited to influence human affairs.

dharma The influence which upholds and supports the universe and living things and empowers evolutionary processes. To live righteously, appropriately, and correctly is to live in accord with its actions. To adhere to a known life-path in accord with the orderly processes of the universe is to fulfill one's personal dharma.

disciple Latin *discipulus*, student, learner; from *discere*, to learn. A disciple is a committed learner-adherent of a philosophical system or spiritual tradition. See *guru*.

ego Mistaken self-identity because of intellectual error and the veiling or clouding of awareness that causes an illusional sense of being separate from God. Inaccurate Self-perception is the basis of egoism. The soul, then presuming itself to be separated from its origins, identifies with fragmented states of awareness. *Egoism* is the condition of being egocentric. *Egotism* is an exaggerated sense of self-importance, usually characterized by arrogance and self-centered willfulness. When the misperception (illusion) of independent self-identity is corrected, the soul, while aware of being individualized, is not confined to or limited by that viewpoint. See *delusion* and *illusion*.

ether Space with fine cosmic forces which are not yet matter but which have the potential to manifest as matter. The other four subtle element influences are air, fire, water, and earth, which interact to express as their corresponding material manifestations. The five subtle element influences are the true essences (*tattwas*) of the manifest universe. Physical manifestation of the elements is said to occur when half of one subtle element influence is mixed with one eighth part of each of the other four subtle element influences.

God The Supreme Being, the Oversoul. The outer manifestation of Consciousness with attributes and qualities, expressing in the direction of universal manifestation.

guna A quality or attribute of Consciousness that regulates nature's forces. The three gunas are the constituent aspects of the whole of nature which determine its actions. *Sattva guna* contributes to order, purity, and luminosity. *Rajas guna* contributes to movement and transformation. *Tamas guna* contributes to heaviness and inertia; its influence clouds the mind and prevails in the material realm. See *maya*.

guru Teacher. That which removes darkness or ignorance of the truth. The light and reality of God is the true guru that removes unknowingness from the mind and awareness of the soul.

heart The physical heart is the hollow muscular organ in the thoracic cavity that pumps blood into arteries to supply the circulatory system. The philosophical meaning is "the vital part of one's being, emotions, and sensibilities; the true Self or soul." When seers advise, "Seek the truth in your heart," they mean that the reality of one's being is to be meditatively contemplated, discovered, and experienced.

heaven Originally a cosmological term used to refer to a region of the universe, which also came to function as a vehicle of religious idealism. In ancient Middle Eastern thought, heaven was imagined as a region of the observable cosmos which pointed beyond itself to a transcendent realm. In ancient Greek mythology, Zeus dwells on Mount Olympus. Writers of the books of The Old Testament referred to heaven as God's abode from which sovereign rule is exercised and to which the faithful righteous are finally welcomed. The New Testament reflects a modified version in which heaven is a creation of God in which God resides, as well as a condition of blessedness experienced by the spiritually prepared. Various sects have their concepts of heaven and its opposite place or condition. Illusion-free understanding allows one to directly know that one's degree of Self-knowledge and God-realization determines personal circumstances.

humility The state of soul awareness when egotism and arrogance are absent.

illusion Misperception: failure or inability to accurately apprehend what is subjectively or objectively observed. Illusions which are believed to be true are delusions which distort awareness and contribute to mental and emotional confusion. When illusions are removed, soul awareness is restored to wholeness. See *ego*, *delusion*, and *tapasya*.

imagination Mental picturing or visualization of that which is not present to the senses. Creative imagination differs from daydreaming or fantasy only in degree. Disciplined imagination enables one to clearly define mental concepts and to envision possibilities of actualizing desired circumstances.

initiation Latin *initium*, beginning; from *inire*, to go in. A rite of passage which admits one into a body of knowledge and the company of adherents of that knowledge. When initiated into kriya yoga practices, the guru or the guru's representative imparts instruction in advanced meditation methods and recommended lifestyle regimens. The disciple, whose soul forces are quickened at the time of initiation, is encouraged to maintain a regular schedule of practice and to nurture mental and spiritual attunement with the gurus of the tradition.

Ishwara Or *Isvara*. The aspect of God which governs and regulates the cosmos.

japa Repetition of a mantra or any of the names of God for the purpose of cultivating devotion and improving meditative concentration. A *japmala* is a string of beads used to count the repetitions and more completely involve the meditator's attention when engaged in prayerful contemplation. The rosary used by devout Catholics serves this purpose.

jivanmukta One who is soul- (*jiva)* liberated (*mukta*) while embodied. Although traces of karma (subliminal mental impressions) may remain, the soul is free because Self-realized. Future actions of the liberated soul are determined by it's innate intelligence, choices, and responsiveness to grace, rather than by karmic compulsion. A *paramukta* (*para*, beyond) is fully liberated, without delusions, illusions, or karmic compulsions. See *salvation*.

jnana (GYA-na) Knowledge, especially knowledge of God.

jyotish The study and application of knowledge of astronomy and astrology. In the *Kaushitaki Brahmana*, an ancient treatise, it is indicated that in 3100 B.C.E. Vedic scholars had knowledge of astronomy used to determine favorable times for religious ceremonies. Vedic astrologers calculate planetary positions in relationship to fixed signs. In this system, certain gemstones are believed to radiate forces similar to those of the major planets, hence the reason for sometimes recommending their use to counteract or to strengthen planetary influences. Ruby is recommended for the influence of the Sun; pearl or moonstone for the Moon; red coral for Mars; emerald for Mercury; yellow sapphire for Jupiter; diamond for Venus; blue sapphire for Saturn; hessonite garnet and chrysoberyl cat's eye for the influences of the north and south nodes of the Moon. The use of gemstones for therapeutic or other helpful purposes should be prescribed by a spiritually enlightened astrologer.

kalpa An Era or duration of time. See *yuga*.

karma Verb-root *kri*, to act; to do; to make [happen]. That which causes effects. Subliminal influences and tendencies, habitual thoughts, mental states, states of consciousness, and actions determine personal experiences. The accumulation of mental and emotional memory impressions (*samskaras*) in the mind and physical body comprise the karmic condition. *Parabdha karma* is the residue of subliminal impressions which may be instrumental in causing future effects. If their potential effects are known to be harmless, they can be allowed to express, thus weakening and exhausting their motive force. They can be neutralized and dissolved by constructive living, surrendered prayer, meditation, repeated superconscious (samadhi) episodes, and the superior force of God-realization. See *samskara*.

kaya-kalpa A regimen for physical and mental rejuvenation and longevity described in Ayurvedic and Siddha Medicine literature. Procedures include routines for internal cleansing and for balancing the governing principles that determine the basic mind-body constitution, prolonged rest, a specific dietary regimen, and extended periods of meditation. To ensure seclusion, the subject usually remains in a quiet dwelling in a natural setting removed from social activities. Vitalizing substances and herbs may be used. Care is taken to provide circumstances which will allow nature's healing forces and the soul's regenerative capacities to be influential. It is reported that by this process some saints have retained their physical bodies for hundreds of years. The most nourishing influences are provided by prolonged, meditative superconscious states. See *Ayurveda* and *rasayana*.

kriya Action, activity, process, procedure. Actions performed to facilitate wellness, success, fulfillment, and clarification of soul awareness. Also, spontaneous, transformative actions which may occur when kundalini energies (*shakti*) are expressive.

kriya yoga *Kriya*, action; *yoga*, to join or unite. Specific lifestyle regimens and meditation practices that restore soul awareness to wholeness.

kundalini Dormant creative energy potential in nature and in the body. When it awakens in nature, life forms emerge and are enlivened. When it awakens in human beings, soul qualities unfold, psychological transformation occurs, intellectual capacities and intuitive powers are improved, exceptional abilities may be acquired, and superconscious and transcendent states may be spontaneously experienced.

Lahiri Mahasaya (Sept.30, 1828 – Sept.26, 1895) Disciple of Mahavatar Babaji and guru of Sri Yukteswar.

Logos The Greek word for the power of Consciousness (Om) considered to be the source of world order and intelligibility which expresses the will (inclination) of God.

love The attracting power of Consciousness that unveils the mind's faculties of perception and releases the soul from bondage to mind and matter. It is common to speak of love of country, love of mankind, love for others, and of love when referring to emotional affection and sentimental attractions. Pure love is healing, redemptive, elicits innate soul qualities, and invites surrender to and participation with the best of all relationships.

Lahiri Mahasaya

mantra *Manas*, mind, that which thinks; *tra*, to protect. A meditation mantra is a potent word, word-phrase, or sound used to focus attention and remove awareness from mental processes, allowing pure consciousness to be directly experienced.

master Latin *magister*, one who is proficient or accomplished. A master of yoga (samadhi) has control over sensory impulses, vital forces, mental states, and states of consciousness.

maya That which measures, defines, limits, and produces forms. The primary substance of nature, the components of which are vibrating creative force (Om), space, time, and cosmic forces which are not yet matter but which can manifest as matter when the actions of the three constituent attributes of nature (*gunas*) are influential. Because of its form-producing inclination, maya is sometimes referred to as Mother Nature. Another characteristic is that of veiling or obscuring the soul's faculties of perception. When a soul identifies with the field of primordial nature, its intuitive and intellectual capacities are blurred or obscured. Maya, although illusory, is not an illusion. It is the substance of everything in the field of objective manifestation. See *guna*.

meditation An uninterrupted flow of attention to an object of concentration. Sustained meditation is contemplation. Meditative contemplation can result in identification of awareness with the object contemplated and realization of pure consciousness.

metaphysics Greek *meta*, beyond; *physika*, physical nature. The branch of philosophy that investigates the primary principles of ultimate reality and the causes of the universe and its aspects and actions.

mind *Manas*, to think; hence *man*, thinker. The information processing organ of human beings and creatures. Cosmic Mind and individualized minds are composed of cosmic forces regulated by the influences of the three primary attributes (gunas) of nature.

moksha Also *mukti*. Liberation of soul consciousness. Accomplished when awareness is devoid of delusions and illusions. See *jivanmukta* and *salvation*.

mudra A "seal," a symbolic gesture. Also a yogic procedure used to enliven the body's life forces and to regulate or acquire mastery over involuntary processes.

nadi A channel through which prana circulates in the body. *Ida* is the left channel along the spinal pathway, the lunar influence. *Pingala* is the right channel, the solar influence. The central channel is *sushumna*, the pathway through which the meditator directs vital forces when practicing some of the kriya yoga meditation techniques or similar procedures. Sushumna is the outermost covering of two subtle astral channels, *vajra* and *chittra*. Within them is *brahmanadi* (the "path of God"), a current of consciousness. When awareness is identified with vajra and chitra nadis, one may have astral perceptions. When awareness is identified with brahmanadi, transcendent samadhi states are possible.

nadi shuddhi Purification of the nadis by pranayama practice or when currents of life force flow spontaneously after kundalini is awakened. See *nadi*, *prana*, and *pranayama*.

Nirguna-Brahma Supreme Consciousness without attributes or qualities. *Saguna-Brahma* is Supreme Consciousness expressing with attributes and qualities.

ojas The refined form of energy that strengthens and vitalizes body and mind and enhances awareness. The final product of food transformation. It is strengthened and increased by stress management, conservation and transmutation of physical and mental energies, mental calmness, wholesome lifestyle routines, spiritual practices, and the cultivation of superconscious states. See *Ayurveda* and *brahmacharya*.

Om (*AUM*) The power of Consciousness emanating from the Godhead which produces all manifestations of nature. The vibration of Om is the primary meditation mantra from which all other mantras derive their potencies.

omnipotence Unlimited power.

omnipresence Present everywhere.

omniscience All knowing.

paramahansa *Para*, beyond, transcendent; *hansa*, swan. One considered to be a spiritual master, a free soul no longer limited by karma or illusions and whose wisdom-impelled actions are always spontaneously appropriate. As a swan has an earthly abode and can soar free in the sky, so a paramahansa dwells in the world but is not confined by it. According to mythology, a swan is able to extract milk from a mixture of milk and water. A paramahansa partakes of the divine essence while living without restrictions in the world.

Paramahansa Yogananda (January 5, 1893 – March 7, 1952). Disciple of Sri Yukteswar and guru of Roy Eugene Davis. His most famous book is *Autobiography of a Yogi*.

prakriti The field of Primordial Nature composed of subtle element influences and their manifestations and characteristics. It is produced and enlivened by the Supreme Being. See *maya*.

Paramahansa Yogananda

prana *Pra*, forth; *an*, to breathe. Life force. Its aspects influence specific life-support functions. The soul's life force flows into the body through the medulla oblongata at the base of the brain. When prana flows freely, health prevails. When flows of prana are weak, imbalanced, or disturbed, physical or psychological discomfort or dysfunction may occur. Pranayama practice harmonizes the flows of prana in the body and allows its expansion. The five aspects of prana in the body are *udana* (upward flowing), seated in the throat, it contributes to speech; *prana*, seated in the chest, it regulates breathing; *samana*, seated in the stomach and intestines, it regulates digestion, assimilation, and biochemical processes; *apana*, seated below the navel, it regulates elimination of waste products; *vyana*, pervades the body and regulates the movements of other aspects of prana. See *pranayama* and *chakras*.

pranayama Freely flowing life force. Pranayama can occur naturally when the mind is calm, or be nurtured by pranayama practice. See *prana*.

Primordial Nature Primary or original nature; Om and its self-referring aspects: space, time, and cosmic forces with potential to express as objective nature. See *prakriti*.

prayer Prayer can be verbal, mental, or the wordless aspiration of the heart (essence of being). Surrendered prayer purifies the ego, allowing apprehension of soul qualities and direct perception of transcendent realities. People of all faiths have experienced the transformational effects of surrendered prayer. Some have realized God by prayer alone, without knowledge or practice of other techniques or procedures. Petitioning prayer is the act of asking God for help or for benefits of some kind, which may manifest as satisfying states of consciousness or desired circumstances in accord with one's faith or recognition.

rasayana Taste, juice, elixir, or essence that circulates to find its natural place, or abode. In Ayurveda, rasayana treatment is a means of restoring the immune system and encouraging body fluids and life forces to circulate and be directed to their natural places. Herbal compounds prescribed for rasayana therapy are many and varied. One such preparation is *chyavanprash*, the food [*prash*] of a sage known as Chyavan who, according to a legendary story, used it to rejuvenate his body after being asked to marry a young woman who was in love with him. One recipe for chyavanprash includes a mixture of raw sugar, clarified butter, Indian gall nut, Indian gooseberry (amla fruit), dried catkins, Indian pennywort, honey, nutgrass, white sandalwood, embrella, aloewood, licorice, cardamom, cinnamon, and turmeric. Ingredients may vary. See *Ayurveda* and *kaya-kalpa*.

reincarnation The doctrine of return, of being born into a physical body after a duration of rest in the astral realm. The belief that the soul can be attracted to the physical realms because its states of consciousness are compatible with them or because of conscious or unconscious mental or emotional attachments. Souls may also move from causal to astral realms. See *astral* and *causal* realms.

renunciation The relinquishment (letting go) of mental and emotional attachments to things, circumstances, emotional states, memories, actions, and the results of actions while being dispassionately involved in relationships, activities, and spiritual practices.

sadhana Verb-root *sadh*, to go straight to the goal. Spiritual self-training and practice.

sage A wise person.

salvation The condition of being liberated from pain or discomfort because of Self-knowledge and the overcoming, removal, or transcendence of karmic conditions, delusions, and illusions by personal endeavor and God's grace. Limited salvation is a confined condition: Self-realization may not be complete or awareness may still be subject to the influences of subliminal impressions. When awareness is removed from all influences that formerly restricted it, liberation is absolute. See *moksha*.

samadhi Verb-root *sam*, to put together. When mental modifications and fluctuations no longer fragment, blur, or disrupt awareness, samadhi (oneness or wholeness) is experienced. Samadhi is a state of clarified awareness. Preliminary samadhi states may be mixed with thoughts, memories, emotions, or fantasies. As mental transformations become less distracting and are calmed, refined samadhi states emerge. Samadhi during which awareness is identified with and supported by an object of meditative contemplation (light, Om, or any other object of attention) is temporary. Samadhi that removes one's awareness from objects is transcendent.

samkalpa Concentrated will power to cause a thing, event, or circumstance to manifest.

samkhya The system of philosophy in which the categories, stages, and orderly processes of cosmic manifestation from the field of pure Consciousness to the physical realm are defined, numbered, classified, and described. *See the philosophy sections of lessons two and three.*

samsara *Sam*, together; verb-root *sri*, to flow. Interactions and transformations occurring in the field of space-time. Unenlightened people involved in the currents of samsara are influenced by its actions. Enlightened souls established in Self-knowledge are not influenced by transitory events and circumstances.

samskara Mental impression, memory. All perceptions of experiences, circumstances, and subjective incidents such as thoughts, feelings, or insights, impress the mind and are retained as memories. If influential, they can disturb mental and emotional peace by causing fluctuations and transformations in one's mind and awareness. They can have potential for pain or pleasure, or be neutral or constructive. Mental impressions made by superconscious influences are entirely constructive. Spiritual practices and superconscious states resist, weaken, and dissolve samskaras. See *karma*.

samyama Perfected meditative contemplation, when concentration and meditation results in identification with the object of contemplation.

sanatana dharma *Sanatana*, eternal; *dharma*, that which supports or upholds. The philosophical system that propounds "the eternal way of righteousness"—the timeless way to live in accord with natural laws and evolutionary impulses which support orderliness, the welfare of all beings, the fulfillment of purposes, and rapid spiritual growth.

Sanskrit The refined, "polished" language from which approximately one hundred Indo-European languages are derived. Prominent in India during the Vedic era and used today by some scholars and truth seekers. The Sanskrit alphabet is considered to be a mantra: a sound-phrase of spiritual significance and power which contains the seed-frequencies of creation. Every sound (*shabda*) has a power (*shakti)* which conveys the sense which is inseparably related to the sound. The sound-element behind the audible sound is the fundamental sound (*sphota*). Contemplation of the subtle sound-element or seed (*bija*) reveals its true essence. Sanskrit mantras are believed to be unique for the purpose of facilitating spiritual awakening. Their potency is derived from Om, the primordial sound current emanating from the Godhead and expressive in the universe. See *Om* and *mantra*.

sat Being, reality, truth, purity, luminosity. Consciousness with attributes may be referred to by its characteristics: *Sat-Chit-Ananda (*Reality-Consciousness-Bliss of Being). See *guna*.

satan Most ancient religions, and most modern ones, imagined and attempted to define a array of unseen presences which affected human life and environmental circumstances: gods, demigods, angels, devils, demons, fairies, and ghosts. Some are considered to be benevolent; others are considered to be harmful. The ancient Hebrew word *satan*, means "obstructor" or "accuser." When the Old Testament was translated into Greek early in the third century B.C.E., *satan* was translated as *diabolus* (French *diable*, German *Teuful*, English "devil"). The first historical endeavor to concentrate all evil in a single personal form occurred before the sixth century B.C.E., in Persia: given the name Ahiriman and described as the Principle of Darkness engaged in ceaseless conflict for control of the world with the Principle of Light. It is likely that the concept of a personified evil influence was adapted from Persian ideas by Jewish religious thinkers and later by early Christians. Truth students who comprehend the categories of God's cosmic manifestations can discern the difference between fact and fiction. God alone exists; *evil* is a misperception (illusion) in regard to misfortune that may be experienced because of lack of knowledge, unwise behavior, or the occasional events that occur because of the transformative actions of nature.

seer That which sees or perceives. One who comprehends the truth of what is observed or analyzed.

Self The soul's true essence of being. See *atman* and *soul*.

Self-realization Conscious knowledge and experience of one's essence of being. The Self of every person and creature is individualized pure consciousness. When identified with mental processes, the body, sensations, and sense objects, the Self becomes outwardly involved and partially forgets its real nature. Self-remembrance, orderly living, spiritual practice, and intellectual and intuitive analysis of one's essence of being facilitates Self-realization: the restoration of awareness to its original, pure state.

shakti Cosmic creative force enlivening nature. Also, the energies of awakened kundalini which vitalize the body and quicken psychological transformation and spiritual growth.

shaktipat The transmission of the energy of the power of Consciousness from one person to another, usually from the guru to a disciple; also its spontaneous awakening because of sustained aspiration to enlightenment, devotion, spiritual practices, and grace.

siddha One who is spiritually perfected or accomplished.

siddhi An exceptional innate power of perception or ability which may emerge along with spiritual growth. Although siddhis may be used to accomplish constructive purposes of all kinds, they should primarily be used to accomplish liberation.

soul A unit of Consciousness (God) which is individualized because of the interaction of the enlivening essence of God and the field of Primordial Nature. When its awareness is blurred it mistakenly presumes itself to be independent of God. This illusional state of awareness has to be clarified to be restored to wholeness. See *salvation*, *moksha*, and *jivanmukta*.

spiritual eye The reflected light of the medulla oblongata at the base of the brain that may be perceived between and behind the eyebrows. The meditator directs attention to and through the spiritual eye to explore refined states of consciousness.

Sri Yukteswar

Sri Yukteswar (May 10, 1855 – March 9, 1936.) A disciple of Lahiri Mahasaya and the guru of Paramahansa Yogananda.

superconsciousness A clarified state of awareness superior to conscious, subconscious, and unconscious states. See *turiya*.

sutra Verb-root *siv*, to sew. Sutras are concise "threads" of ideas or concepts spoken or written to communicate information.

swami A member of the ancient monastic order reorganized by the philosopher-seer Adi (the first) Shankara in the seventh century. A swami renounces all mundane attachments, selflessly works for the highest good of others, and (usually) engages in spiritual practices.

tantra *Tan*, to extend or expand. Tantric philosophy explains the processes of creation and dissolution of the cosmos, procedures for relating to universal forces and accomplishing the aims of life, how to awaken and express innate abilities, and meditation techniques to clear the mind and facilitate awakening to ultimate Truth-realization.

tapasya From the verb-root *tap*, to burn. Disciplined practices which result in psychological transformation and the removal of restrictions to spiritual growth and Self-actualization.

tattva The true essence of a thing which can be known by practicing *samyama*: meditative contemplation.

Transcendental Field Pure Consciousness, the Absolute.

turiya The fourth state of consciousness transcending the three ordinary states of deep sleep, the dream state, and ordinary waking states. See *superconsciousness*.

Upanishads *Upa*, near; *ni*, down; *sad*, to sit. A collection of texts considered sacred, with origins in oral traditions. Centuries ago, in India, the disciple would live in the guru's ashram and "sit near" to learn. Among the several Upanishads, those which are more widely published are referred to as the principle ones because of their general accessibility. Several less known Upanishads contain specific yogic instruction. One such text, *Shandilya Upanishad*, was written by an ancestor of Lahiri Mahasaya.

vasana Latent tendency, a subconscious impulse which causes thought-waves to arise in the mind, mental transformations, and fluctuations in awareness. They can be neutralized by constructive living, spiritual practices, and superconsciousness (samadhi). See *vritti*.

veda Revealed or directly perceived knowledge. Vedic texts are records of insights of ancient seers; the Upanishads elaborate on the Vedas.

Vedanta The summing up of the wisdom of the Vedas: one Reality is the essence of all that exists.

vritti Movement, wave, fluctuation, or modification occurring in the mind and awareness impelled by *vasanas* (impulses of the subliminal tendencies of samskaras) which stir them into motion. Vrittis are calmed by dispassionate observation of circumstances and by meditation practiced to the stage of superconsciousness. See *vasana*.

Vyasa A name used by several sages who gathered and arranged many of the Vedic texts.

yama-niyama *Yama*, restraint. The resisting and regulating of destructive impulses and habits by decisive choice and will power, and replacing them with opposite characteristics: harmlessness; truthfulness; honesty; constructive use of vital forces and soul capacities; and insightful renunciation which makes possible appropriate relationships and prudent use of natural resources. *Niyama*, not-restraint, the constructive actions: maintaining inner and outer cleanliness or purity; nurturing soul contentment in all circumstances; disciplined practice to facilitate psychological transformation; study and meditative contemplation to awaken to Self-knowledge and higher realities; and surrender of the illusional sense of selfhood in favor of awakening to Self- and God-realization.

yantra A symbolic geometrical drawing used as a focus for meditative contemplation that depicts the actions and influences of cosmic forces. Favored by many yogis is *Sri Yantra*, composed of circles, triangles, lotus petals, and mantras within a square that contains the energies. The design symbolically portrays the interactions of *Shiva* and *Shakti*: Supreme Consciousness and its creative powers.

Sri Yantra

yoga 1. To "yoke" or "unify." To bring together, to identify with the One Consciousness by using specific practices that remove restrictions from the mind and awareness. 2. Any of the various systems used for this purpose. 3. Samadhi, the meaning used in Patanjali's Yoga-Sutras. See lesson five, *The Fundamentals of Yoga*.

yuga An era or designated duration of time. Centuries ago, vedic astronomer-seers taught a theory of time-cycles to explain the effects of cosmic forces on human beings and evolutionary trends that affect Planet Earth. The ascending cycle is one-half of a complete 24,000-year cycle: a 1,200-year Dark Age *(Kali Yuga,* a time-period of confusion) during which most human beings are intellectually deficient and spiritually unaware; a second *(Dwapara)* 2,400-year era during which intellectual powers and spiritual awareness increase and electric and magnetic properties of nature are discovered anew; a third *(Treta)* 3,600-year era when intellectual powers are keen and knowledge of nature's forces is common; a 4,800-year era of enlightened truth *(Satya)* perception during which many on the planet can comprehend the reality of God. We are currently in the early stages of a second ascending 2,400-year era which emerged in 1700 and will continue until the year 4,100 when a 3,600-year ascending Mental Age will begin. The duration of the Ages, in ascending order, are actually 1,000, 2,000, 3,000, and 4,000 solar years. An additional ten percent of the duration of each Age begins and ends each transition phase.

This calculation of time-cycles is based on the theory that forces from the center of our galaxy influence the electromagnetic field of the solar system and the mental and intellectual faculties of its human inhabitants. When our solar system is distant from the galactic center, human powers of perception and intellect are weak, soul awareness is obscured, and ignorance of the facts of life prevail. When our Sun and its planets are nearest to the galactic center, human powers of perception are refined, intellectual abilities are pronounced, soul knowledge is more easily unveiled, and various degrees of enlightenment are common.

Regardless of the Age in which one lives, when aspiration to Self-discovery is impelling, spiritual growth that culminates in illumination of consciousness is possible. One can choose to awaken from identification with characteristics which are common to the individual deluded condition to the stage which makes possible comprehension of fine forces behind the outer appearance of nature. At this stage one can appreciate the philosophical principles upon which kriya yoga practices are based and be motivated to right living and spiritual endeavor. Further awakening enables one to apprehend and effectively relate to Cosmic Mind. The final awakening is the result of spontaneous revelation of innate knowledge.

Because of a mistake that was made several centuries ago (approximately 700 B.C.E.) in calculating the progressions of the yugas, many people still erroneously believe that we are currently in a Dark Age cycle that will continue for several hundred thousand years. The error occurred near the end of the last descending Dwapara Yuga. Astrologers, not wanting to inform the public about the impending emergence of two consecutive Dark Ages (a 1,200 year descending era followed by an ascending era of equal duration) proclaimed that the Dwapara Yuga would continue. Much later, the mistake was noted, but its cause was not then known.

Observation of the state of collective human consciousness and of scientific discoveries and technological advances during the past two hundred years indicates that the current era is one of rapid intellectual and spiritual awakening characteristic of an emerging Dwapara (second) Yuga.

Roy Eugene Davis began his discipleship training with Paramahansa Yogananda in Los Angeles, California, in 1949, when he was eighteen years of age. After being ordained by his guru in 1951, he served as the minister of the Self-Realization Fellowship Church in Phoenix, Arizona (1952 – 1953). After two years in the United States Army Medical Corps, Mr. Davis began to teach and write. He has lectured and presented meditation seminars in more than 100 North American cities, Japan, Brazil, Europe, and West Africa. Some of his books have been published in nine languages in eleven countries.

Recommended Supplemental Reading

Books by the author.

The Path of Light*
A guide to 21st century discipleship and spiritual practice in the kriya yoga tradition. Includes all of the verses of Patanjali's yoga-sutras.
Hardcover, 160 pages, $7.95

The Self-Revealed Knowledge That Liberates the Spirit
The soul's sojourn in time and space and its awakening from ordinary states of awareness to illumination of consciousness.
Hardcover, 160 pages, $7.95

The Eternal Way*
The Inner Meaning of the Bhagavad Gita.
Hardcover, 320 pages, $14.95

An Easy Guide to Ayurveda*
The natural way to wholeness.
Softcover, 160 pages, $4.95

The Spiritual Basis of Real Prosperity
How to always be in the flow of resources and supportive events and relationships for your highest good.
Hardcover, 160 pages, $7.95

A Master Guide to Meditation*
The natural process clearly explained.
Hardcover, 128 pages, $6.95

Una Guía Maestra para la Meditación
Spanish edition of *A Master Guide to Meditation*
Softcover, 142 pages, $4.95

English language editions of these titles* are also published in India.
Information will be provided on request.

Center For Spiritual Awareness

The international headquarters of Center for Spiritual Awareness is located on eleven secluded acres in the north Georgia mountains, 90 miles northeast of Atlanta. Facilities include offices and publishing department, the main sanctuary with an attached dining room where vegetarian meals are served during retreats, the Shrine of All Faiths Meditation Temple, two library buildings, a bookstore, and six comfortable guest houses for retreat participants.

Retreats, during which the philosophical principles and practices of kriya yoga are taught, are offered from early spring until late autumn. Special retreats are occasionally provided for members. Seminars are scheduled each year in cities in North America and in other countries. Meditation groups are active in several communities. *Truth Journal* is published bimonthly. *Radiance* magazine is published for kriya initiates.

Our parent corporation was chartered in the state of Georgia in 1964. The 501(c)(3) nonprofit tax number is 58-0942053. Funding is provided by our members and by individuals who benefit from our services, donations made at seminars and retreats, and sale of books and other teaching aids. Our seminars and retreats are always offered on a donation basis.

Our purpose is to provide practical, helpful information for the spiritual education of all interested persons. Although we are not formally affiliated with any other organization, we cooperate with many individuals and groups with whom we share philosophical ideals.

We affirm that it is possible, by right personal endeavor and God's grace, for all truth seekers to have a conscious relationship with the Infinite, fulfill life's purposes in harmony with natural laws, and creatively express their innate potential.

Center For Spiritual Awareness
P.O. Box 7 · Lakemont, Georgia 30552-0001 (U.S.A.)
Telephone (706) 782-4723 Office hours weekdays 8 a.m. – 4 p.m.
Fax (706) 782-4560 e-mail address csainc@csa-davis.org
Internet Web Site www.csa-davis.org

The CSA offices and retreat center are located off Lake Rabun Road in Rabun County.
Travel directions will be provided on request.